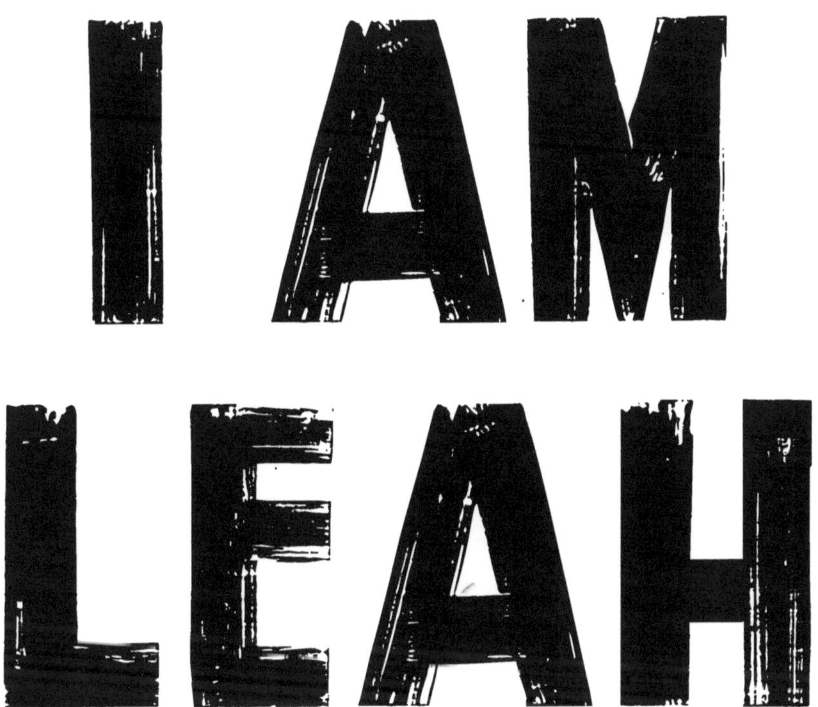

by

Leah Keith

Visit our website at **www.StillwaterPress.com** for more information.

First Stillwater River Publications Edition

ISBN-13: 978-1-95033947-1

1 2 3 4 5 6 7 8 9 10
Written and illustrated by Leah Keith
Published by Stillwater River Publications, Pawtucket, RI, USA.

For my family,
My sister, Melissa Keith, my father, Robert Keith,
my mother, Deborah Coury, and my step-father, Fred Coury,

Thank you for always believing in me.

FOREWORD

Leah has a voice and she wants you to know it. She wants you to hear her before you decide who she is. She wants you to see her and take the time to get to know her before you think you already do. She will surprise you with her unique wisdom and colorful sense of humor. She is not what you expect her to be. She is proud of who she is and she makes no apologies for it. In this book, Leah uses her voice in the form of poetry and art. These are her true and unedited words spoken out loud to her great friend and support person Stephen Alfano. Steve has also assisted her during many art classes at the Rhode Island School of Design, sponsored by the VSA of RI. Leah paints free hand with acrylic paint on canvas. She has developed her own style using bold colors in sweeping strokes. Her work is abstract and seems to be a form of meditation for her. When painting, she is very focused and often appreciates pure silence. After completing a painting, this is usually the time she recites a poem from her head spontaneously. This artistic process is done at her studio at 30 Cutler Street in Warren, RI. Here is the place-where she shows her art and sometimes performs her poetry during Bristol/Warren Art Nights or special Holiday events.

Leah has won the Allen Ginsberg Award for outstanding poetry through the VSA of RI three times, and was chosen to represent them as their Poet Laureate for the past three years. As the Poet Laureate, she has been given themes to write about and read her poems at certain events such as, the celebration of the 25th Anniversary of the Americans with Disabilities Act at the Pawtucket, Rhode Island Town Hall.

When Leah was born in 1987 we didn't know what to expect, but the available information at the time was pretty dismal. Only 10 years before, parents who had a child born with Down syndrome were often told by doctors to put them in institutions at birth, because they would be a burden to the family. They may never walk or talk, and other siblings in the household would be brought down by them. This is what parents were often being told when their beautiful and precious baby was born—"put them away and forget about them." This was criminal and there is nothing further from the truth.

Leah has taught me, her mother, more about life than any other person or experience in my life and I am so grateful to have the experience of raising her. She is more wise and emotionally intelligent than anyone I know. She understands what is truly important, is incredibly intuitive, and is a gifted poet and artist. She is unabashedly herself, is fully confident, and makes no apologies for her differences. Leah says, "I am different and different is good."

At the same time, I can't say her life has been very easy. She has often felt isolated and withdrawn and feared the bullying that she witnessed against others with intellectual differences. She learned to keep quiet and was often afraid to advocate for herself as a child. Although she was extremely articulate and had a tremendous vocabulary, people would automatically assume that she was just this loving, sweet child who had little to say and just wanted to hug. People had no idea how much she resented this assumption and still does to this day.

Leah was always creative and the writing was on the wall from an early age, quite literally, that she would aspire to be a published author and artist. As a young child she would experiment with all mediums and there wasn't an empty spot on the walls, floor, or book pages where she didn't write, draw, and paint using anything she could try, including toothpaste, shaving cream, and all kinds of food products as well as permanent markers, crayons, and paint. After a few years we were able to get her to limit her great works to paper and canvas.

Leah was always adventurous and fearless and would often leave the house unattended at all times day or night to go out and explore the world. Luckily we lived in a safe place with wonderful neighbors and Leah always made it home without harm. However, her mother and father were a bit traumatized during this time and gained many gray hairs.

Leah always had a unique wisdom and intuition. She would often know when someone was pregnant before they did and know the sex of the baby. Leah would sometimes answer my thoughts out loud or know things about people she just met.

For instance, one amazing story is when new neighbors moved in and we went over to introduce ourselves. Leah was about 6 years old and our new neighbor had just told Leah and I that his name was Pat. Leah kept looking up at him and saying, "David". Over and over I would tell Leah, "His name is Pat, say Pat." When our new neighbor realized Leah was calling him David he was shocked and told us that everyone calls him Pat, but it was really his middle name. His first name was David!

After Leah graduated high school she went to college at Bristol Community College in Fall River, MA, and studied theater. She performed in many plays and even helped to write pieces for different skits. She played a beggar in *Treasure Island* and a thug in a modern production of *Measure for Measure* by Shakespeare. She made many friends there and felt like she had found a place where she fit in. High school in Barrington, RI hadn't been a place of acceptance for her. She was often separated from her peers in a self-contained classroom where she felt embarrassed. When she joined the theater there she was never included and was usually left to just watch from the sidelines. She often felt invisible and that no one understood who she was or took the time to get to know her. So when she got to experience theater in college it was exhilarating and she began to come out of her shell when others could see who she really was and how much she had to offer.

Leah has an unusual knowledge about people and she often knows immediately when someone walks in a room if something is bothering them, even if she is meeting them for the first time. As she has gotten older I believe she learned to suppress some of these special gifts in order to fit in, but although Leah learns differently than others and some skills are harder for her, she also has special gifts that others don't. Leah has a unique understanding of what's important and she will remind you that dwelling on a past event or holding a grudge can be a poor use of time and emotion. She always reminds me to see the positive in a situation and often helps me make sense of other people's behaviors and not to take things personally. I feel so fortunate that I get to be her mother!

–Deborah Coury

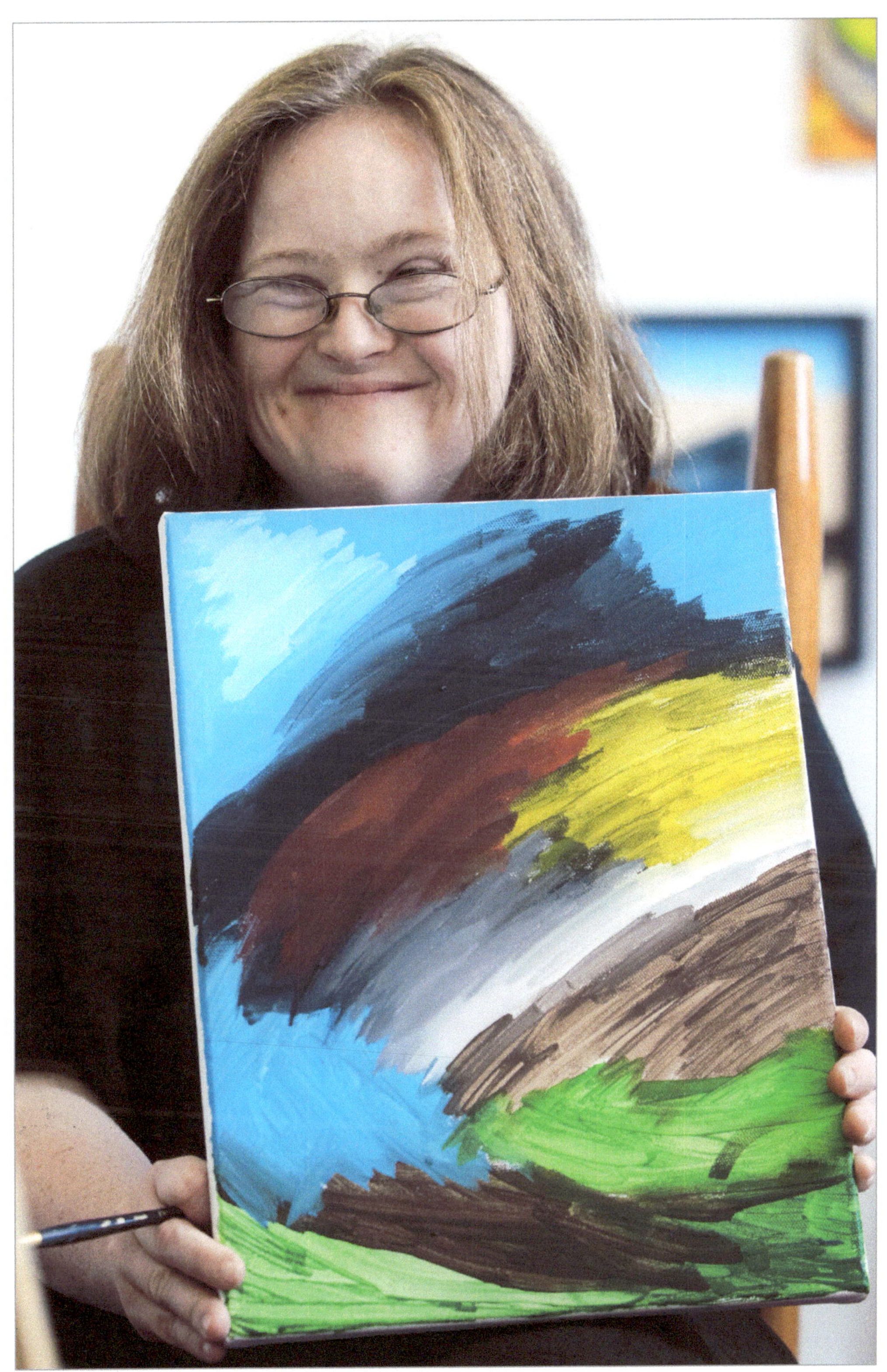

ACKNOWLEDGEMENTS

First and foremost I want to thank Stephen Alfano for being my good friend and supporting and encouraging me through my artistic process.

Thank you to Dawn and Steve Porter at Stillwater River Publications for believing in me and working so hard to get this book done.

Thank you to Martha Lavieri and Jeannine Chartier at the VSA for providing me with great opportunities to learn about art and poetry.

I want to thank my great teacher and theater director, Rylan Brenner, at BCC who included me in every aspect of theater and helped me gain confidence and believe in myself.

Thank you to Sue Babin and the Rhode Island Developmental Disabilities Council for the grant that made this book possible.

Thank you to Jay MacKay for being my friend, fellow artist and encouraging me to explore new opportunities that lead me to accomplish my dream of publishing this book.

This book is in memory of Mark Robidoux, my good friend who hung out with me every weekday afternoon for many years, walking Finn, cooking great meals and doing "stuff and things, and things and stuff."

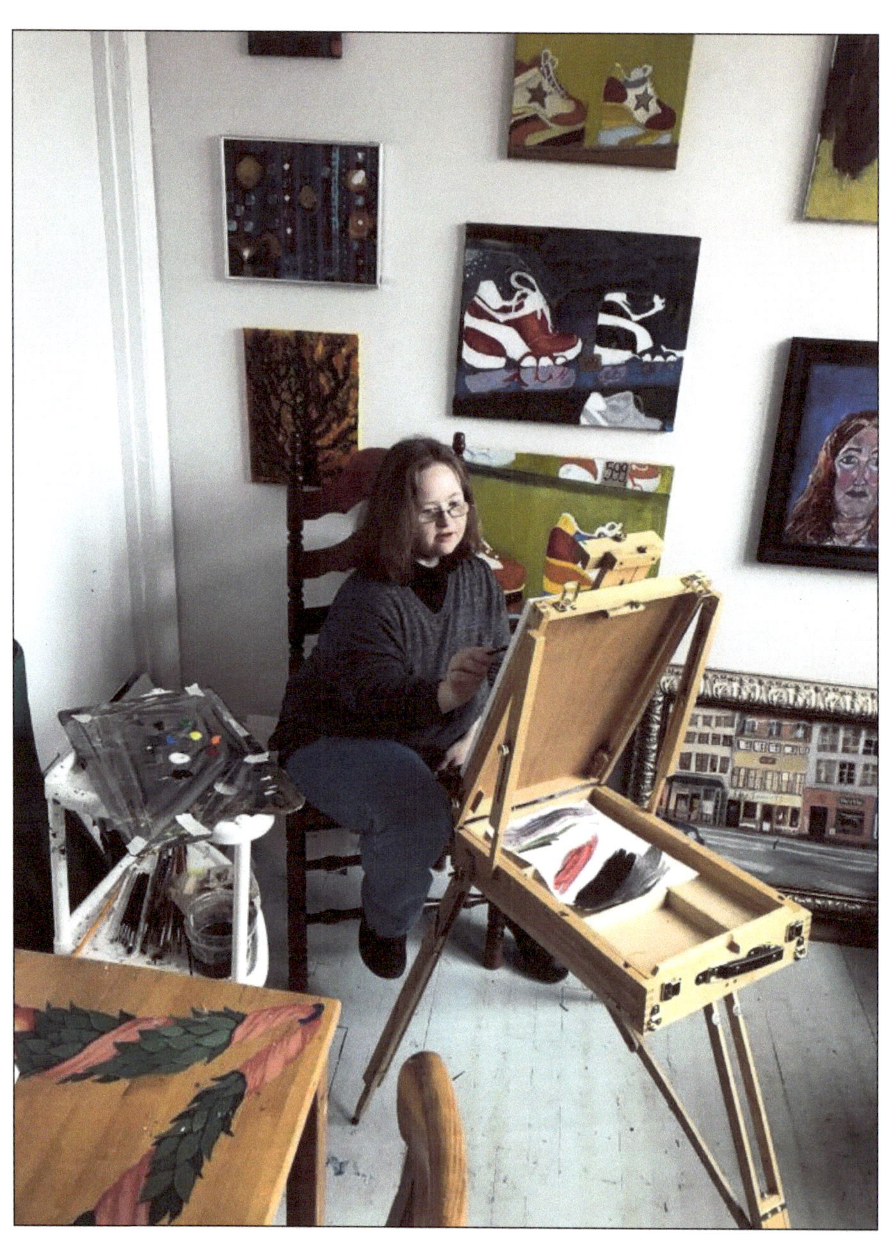

INTRODUCTION

I would like to put, into the best words I know, the summation of what I believe to be the heart of my sister's message which includes her purpose here, what she means to the rest of us, and what she means to me. It is ultimately all love, but I would like to expound.

Being different is good. Diversity is something we need to appreciate. Standing out is a blessing. Those who remind us of ourselves, our vulnerability, our victim consciousness, and mirror our shadow aspects; they are our hidden heroes. They are placed in front of us to gift all that has ceased to be expressed from our spirit thus far. It is our responsibility to release the blocks of our ego so we may see them.

My sister is filled with love for everyone; she is accepting and gracious without judgement. Like water, she is strong and eternal. From her I have only seen kindness; a gentle disposition that is subtle and understated yet deeply rooted in earthly wisdom.

My sister's wisdom may go astray at times, but only in the external world. She has always been present with her internal truth, building on it each day. My privilege in writing this message for her is really for myself; to have my love and admiration of her artistic capacity and expressive heart documented so she may share this message with you. The message is one of living in our hearts and being true to ourselves every moment of everyday. I believe Leah does this naturally. She has travelled beyond the depth of her ego and into the depths of her heart and soul, where she brings back the beautiful, bountiful, infinite joy and wisdom of our natural world. Once we have gotten out of our own way, this is profoundly calm and reassuring. It is the comfort of our eternal true selves.

Succumb and surrender. This is the action my sister's words provoke in me. Not to just bring my attention to a halt in serenity, but to sink into it. Her poetry and art have the power to surround me in an eternal validating loving presence. I love it so much, as does she. My love for her light is reflected so brightly in her expression.

She is a quiet hero to anyone who seeks to be their own best friend. Always having the courage and power to be her own best ally, coming from within, she thrives.

She has helped me discover parts of myself I didn't believe were there. I read her words and wonder where she gets her inspiration. Deeply, I know it is from the same eternal source we all seek to return to, yet she flies there effortlessly. Though I know it may not always feel this way to her, it is how I have grown to see her powers. It's a subtle presence; I am in awe of her mind. Everything current in my life is so eloquently described in her poems. It is validating. They make me feel real and believe that I'm made of magic, worth believing in it, and humbled.

There is much thought around how to use our power. Leah, in contrast, doesn't need to use her power at all. She has embodied the art of getting out of one's mind and into the heart her whole life. She simply is powerful, and it is my great duty as her sister to help her bring this to the eagerly awaiting audience I know she can reach and who want to reach her.

My sister's writing makes me feel in touch with my heart. I hope it does the same for you

–Melissa Keith

PROLOGUE

Leah Keith is not always in a good mood. She's dynamic and complex, like all people are. When I first met Leah, she was interested in taking up painting. We'd meet every Wednesday at 1:30 to paint with acrylics, and she was almost immediately uninhibited with expressiveness (a courageous vulnerability many artists struggle with). Her unique perspective, imagination, and application of mediums, are primary qualities within the arena of art. This free-flow of creativity led to many, many paintings—all interesting, with an evolving style as she developed her technique. We would talk here and there, not often. Eventually we got into philosophical topics, existentialism… deep stuff. I forget exactly what was said, but I knew that I had to write it down. When something is truly unique, it is recognizable. I suggested that we try some freestyle poetry, Leah was familiar with the idea and agreed. Her expressiveness flowed with the same courageous spirit her painting did, and I did all that I could to keep up. Poetry became part of the routine, and Leah has continued to express herself with a stream of consciousness style that still amazes me. I feel honored to help create conditions for Leah to express herself without restriction, continuing to transcend limitations.

–Stephen Alfano

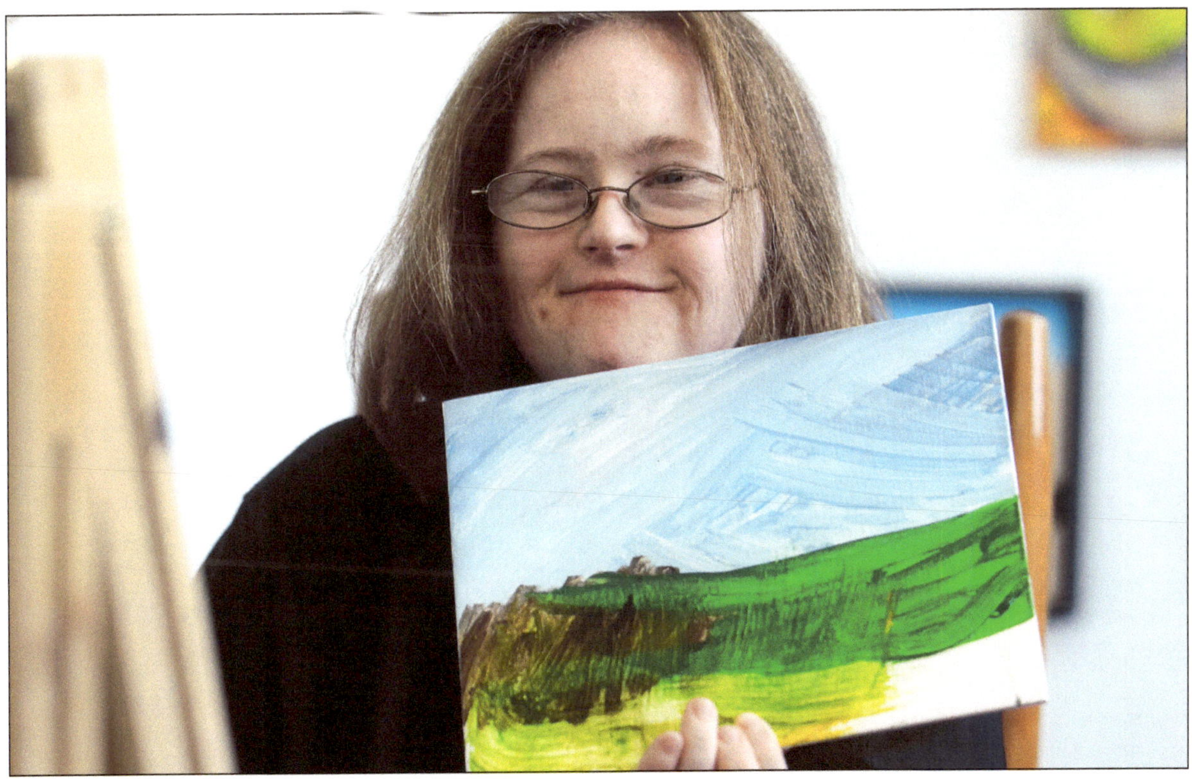

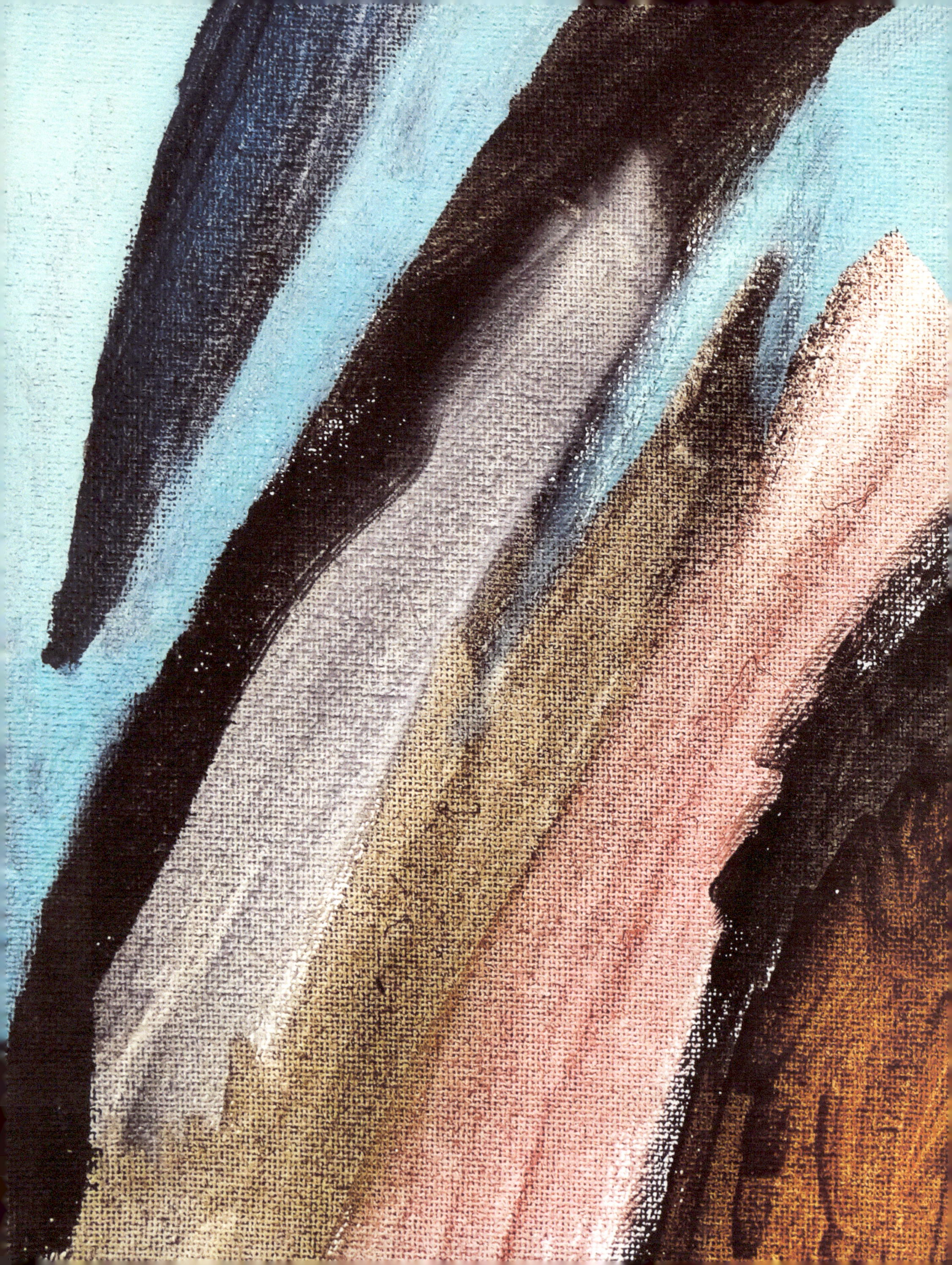

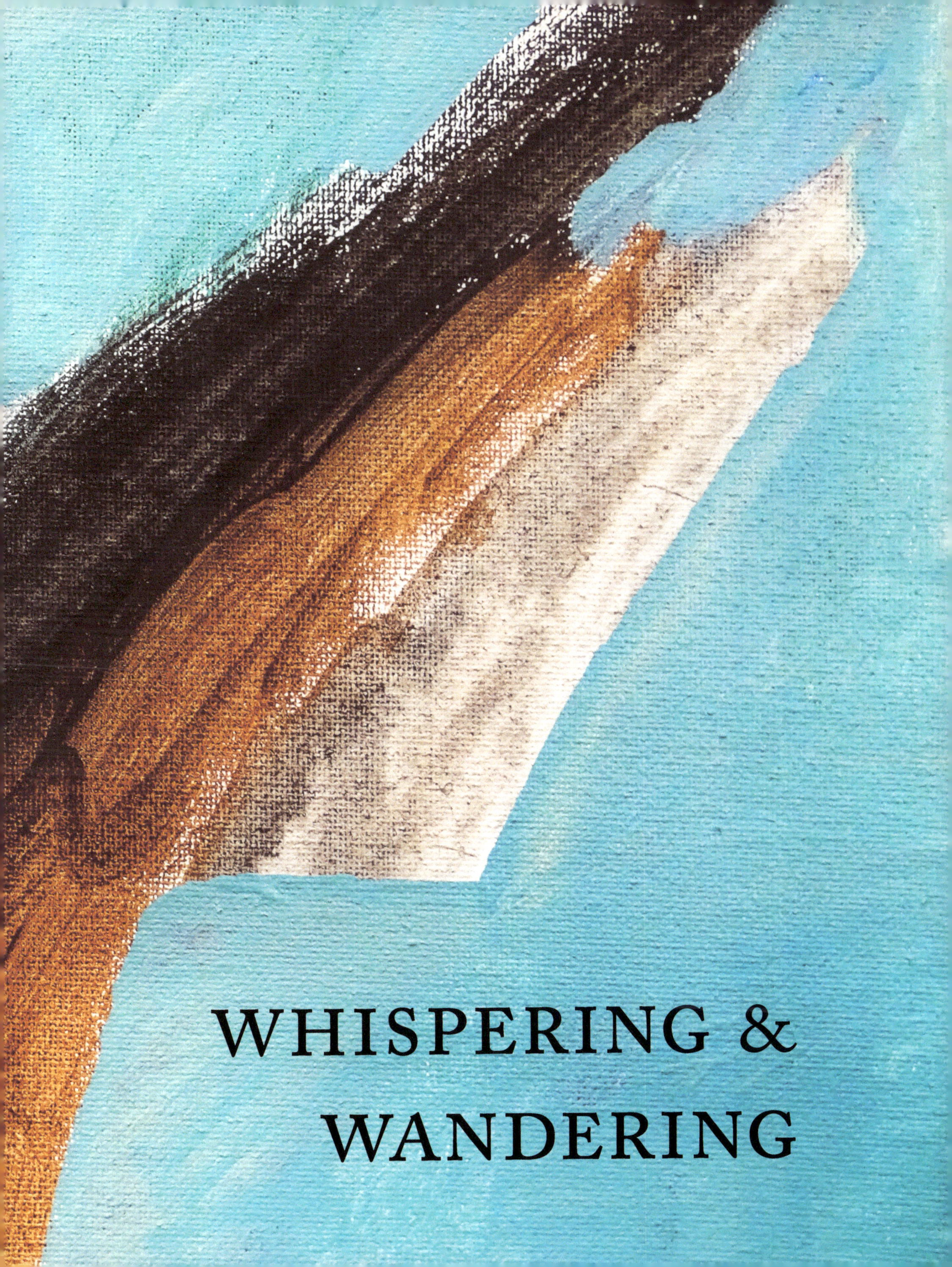
WHISPERING &
WANDERING

Wandering and Whispering

The wandering eyes of a whispering
silently,
peacefully,
of a dream
and movement
like it's own surrounding
of that blank space
like a hole,
that completely dark sky
that falls into place like dust,
like the rain
and how it forms
by itself.
Like eyes of SOUL & LIFE & more
than anything
like behind it.
Like many many of years,
just keeps rolling and rolling
like a clock
like out of space
and years before that
that we never have known before
than anything like this moment
like you already know what's going to
happen NEXT,
and of that life—
or is it just being alive?
And like this shadow in the dark
like an eye of an eagle, or a RAVEN
that goes OUT THERE
Forever like a dream
and in that dream
like with everything is just pretend
and yours
kind of like another world
that you never had seen
because it's creating itself
over AGAIN
like the trees and the ocean.
Part of that dream
that you never had known before
nothing but SILENCE
of movement, but STILL.
But does it really matter?
OR IS IT...
Just something else
like of this epic, blue moon
That stays right there forever, of that daylight
just like of that last summer ago
and in this little town
with so many secrets
or is it just a little bit more?
Like a disguise of yourself
that you can't un-recognize
and without like a pair of hearts, or is it
just more?
Like spirits that you can remember
and never more.
And doesn't miss that
and of color
because that is what it is:
A BIG MEMORY
or a blur
of ANYTHING

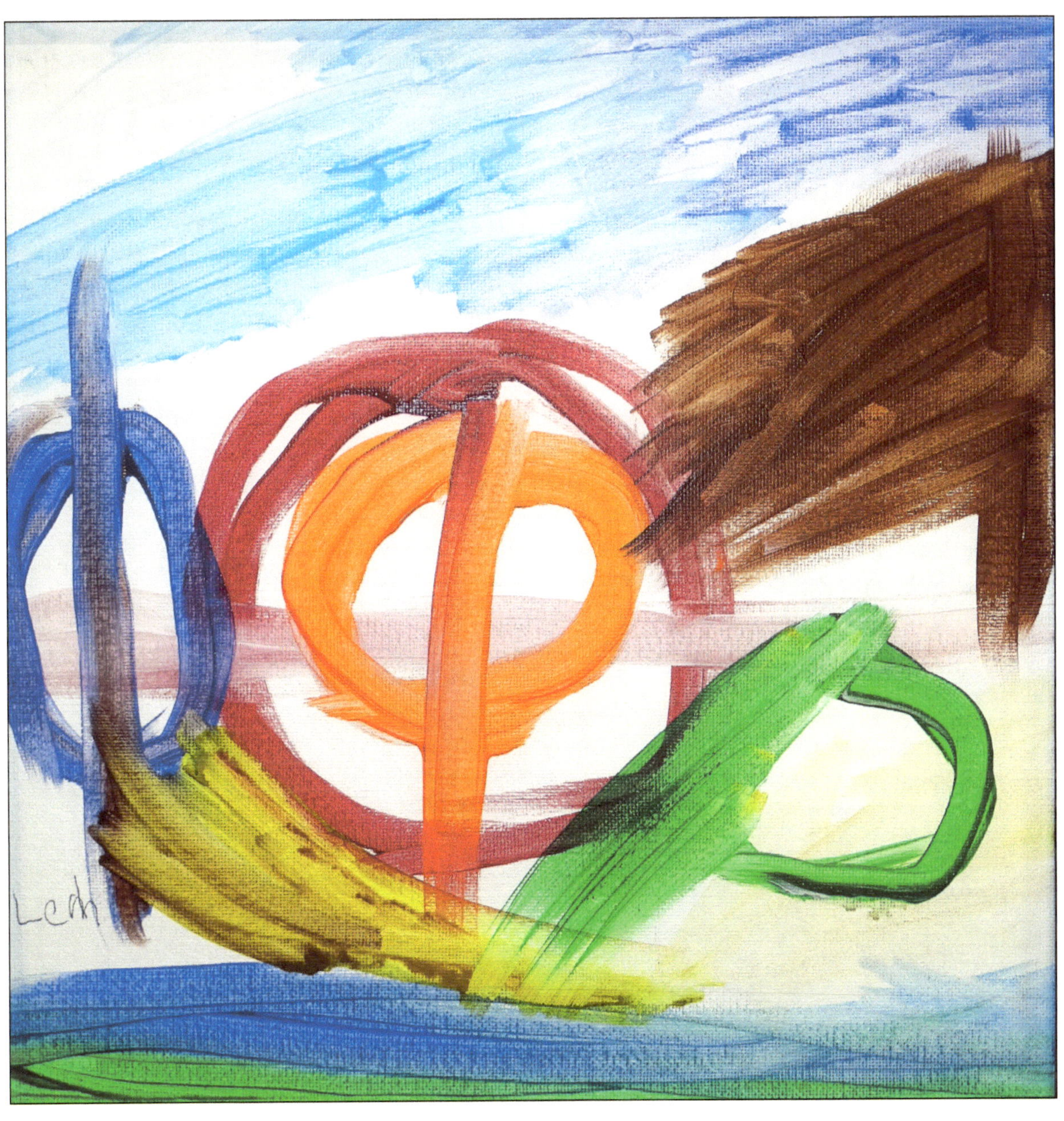
Lch

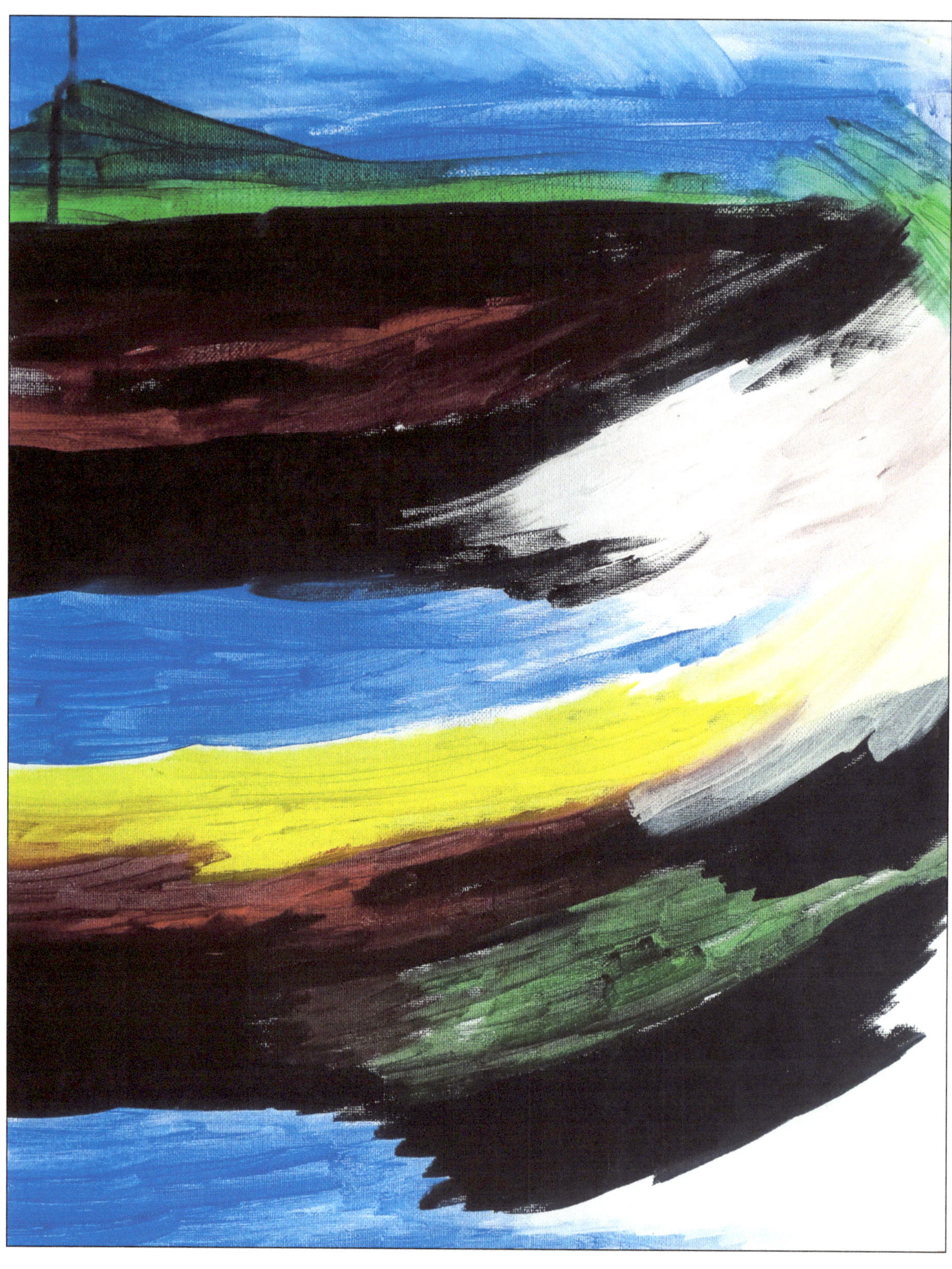

II

Treacherous setting, peacefully
Of dreams
Like fantasizing of this moment of life
Like a midnight slumber,
Whispering until dawn,
Of awakening sacrifice
Like beyond awakening of this daily life
That's been hundreds of years, and more
Within and without, and more beyond
Of this remembering dream,
That you meant not to be, or not to be that question
Like this unknown creature of the other side
Of that life of fantasy
That you will know, but with time
Even that sacred, whispering, secret thing
Has never been solved
Like it will be forever.

The Midnight Whisperer

Of this night of slumber
In that memory and this
Dream of the midnight moon
The dark sky—like the awakening moment
A moment like reason
And this raven
That flies in the dark
Like a broken heart
Likely of this awakening moment in time
Like everything and everything else
That happens
So quickly—but slow
Like the wind—that you don't see
But it is there—but you can't hear it
And it's completely raining
Like a rainy night—of this, and more
And everything surrounding
Like this one night—particular night
Of Hollow's Eve
And not this whispering diary
That burns out into flame

Like this beyond mystery
And of before and of this
Very first Hallow's Ever Harvest
And that life—everything
That we never have seen
Like dark shadows
And the eyes of souls
And in that night
All these people that live in that
Little town and in this secret little town,
And of their village
And what they have known for
Like behind of secrets
Like it's gonna be different
Than what they had before this moment
And this reason—and without
There is gonna be this night
When this other particular someone
That they don't even know
Moving there—in that town
Like everything is going to change
Everything and everyone

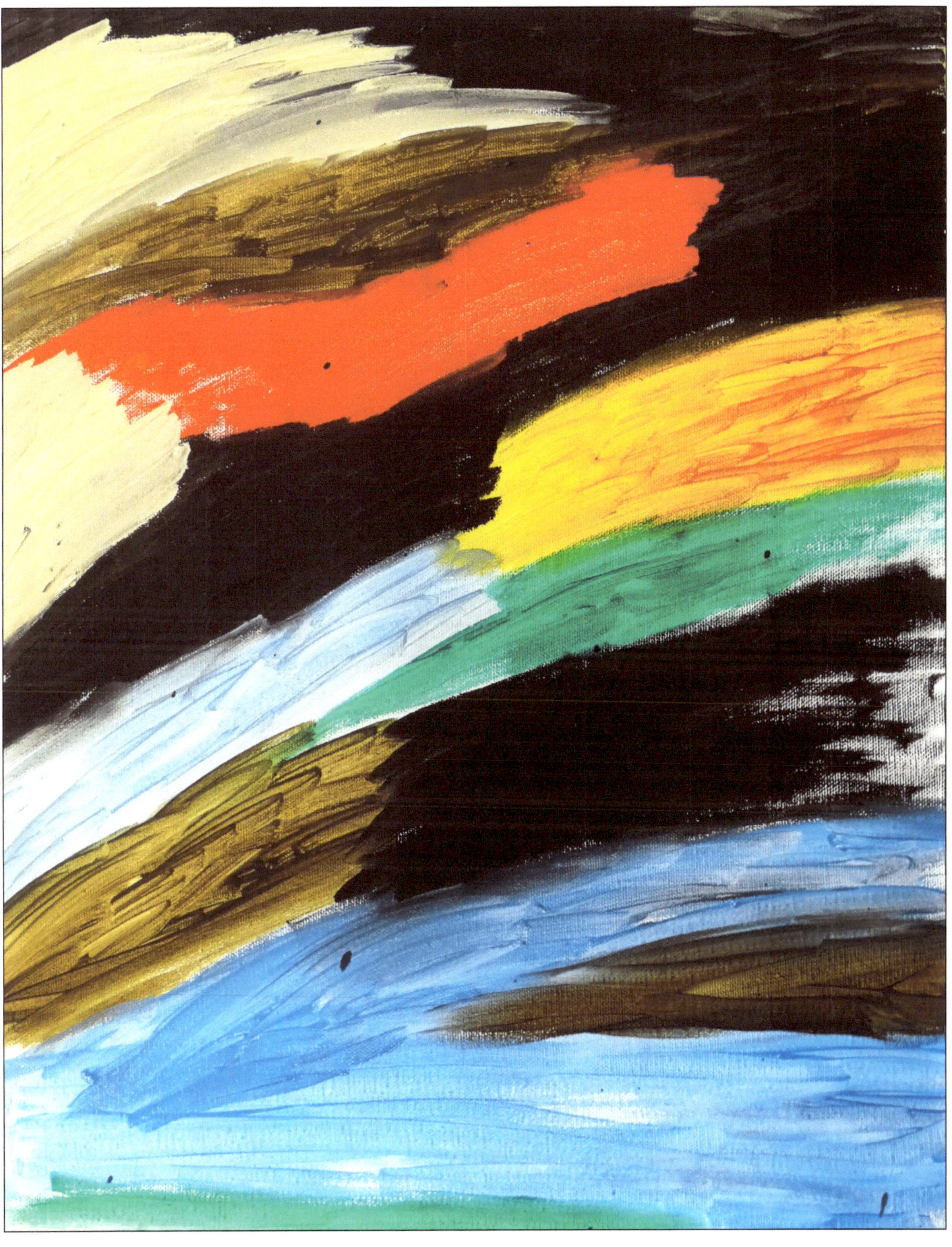

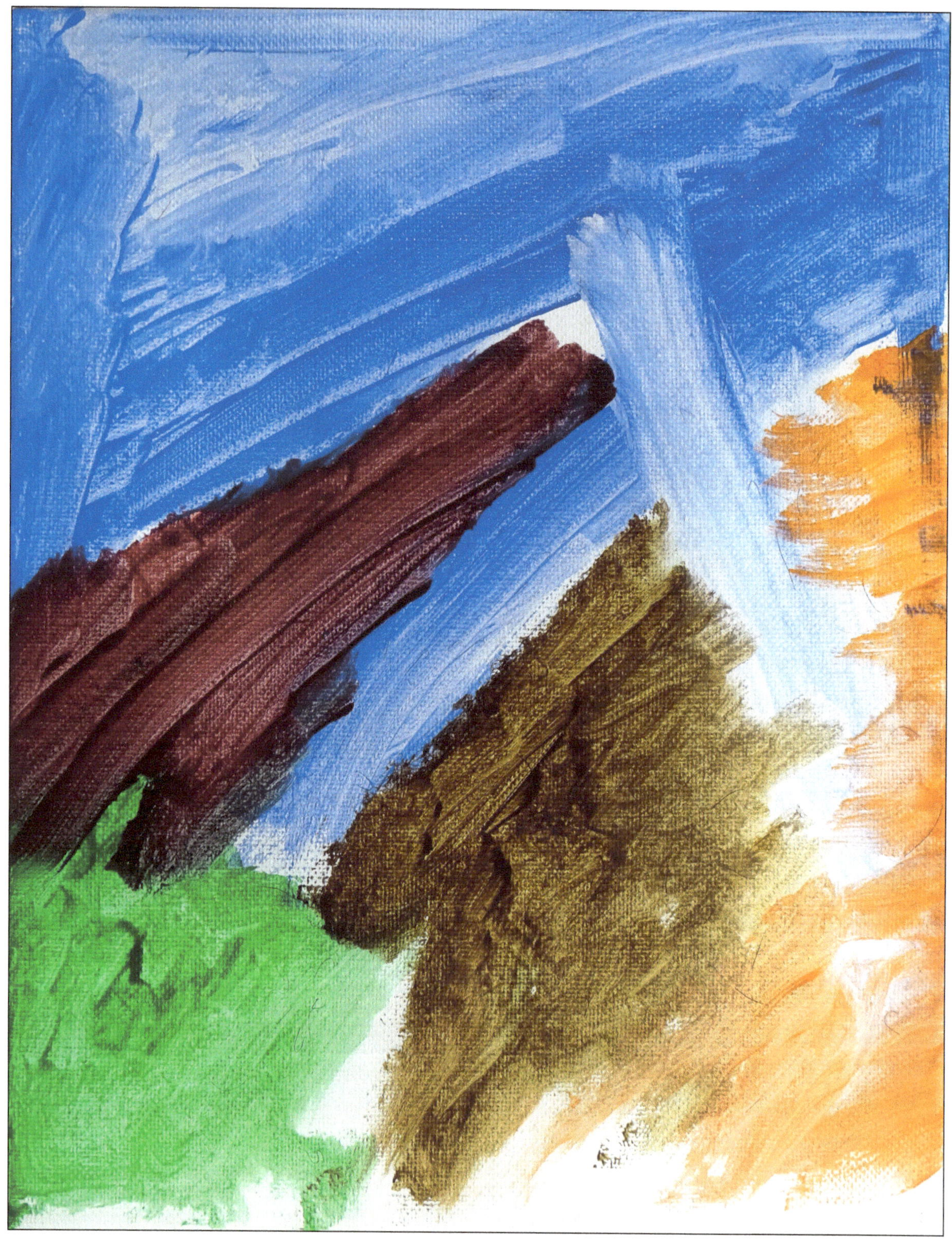

The Whispering Keeper

The voice of whispering
Out there in the wind
Setting—like out there—in the dark
Of like the daylight,
Mystery of silence
And of this whispering voice
That you could never hear
Until now...
The silence that makes you want to scream
But it could make you really crazy
So fast
Or not
Or is it really because of this moment in time?
Even in life—as itself
The keeper of the flame, of movement
Like an angel in the sky,
That you could never see
And of your shadow of your own pair of eyes
The eyes of souls—like a big part of you
Is still there, and you're watching
Things all around you, even people like that
Could never really see you
But you can hear them
Like a dream world that you're in
Like you're out there—in the desert,
so peacefully
I've been running all my life—
Even with circles in my head and in my mind...
Even more, in this life
As I know—so suddenly—something that I
could never
Like my voice—a voice of reason
Desperately—and in time, like it's been
that summer
And years ago—that was really about
But what is it really about?
But in this dream
That is a dream
Is like continuing and going
Like you go places, like you've never had
done before
And like fearness that you never even tried
Because sometimes, I think
Like fear itself
Like a big act of listening
Like it was before—of anything that can
be possible
Remembering memory—I remember a lot
of things
But things that I could do
The things that I never thought of before

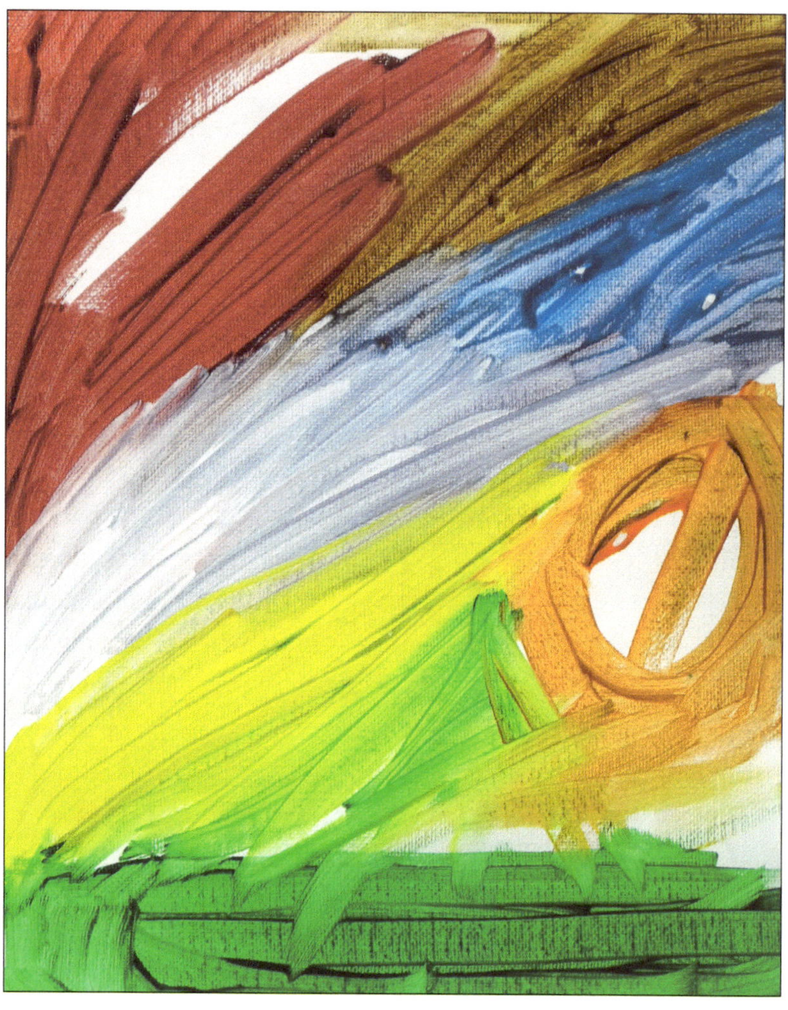

The wandering eyes
Looking through the breaking,
    whispering glass
Of this mirror frame
Like a shadow that you see
    faced at you
And parts of this memory
Like a dream—of silence
Like the movement of the wind
And more—of this—in reason
Or without—of that
And this moment of time

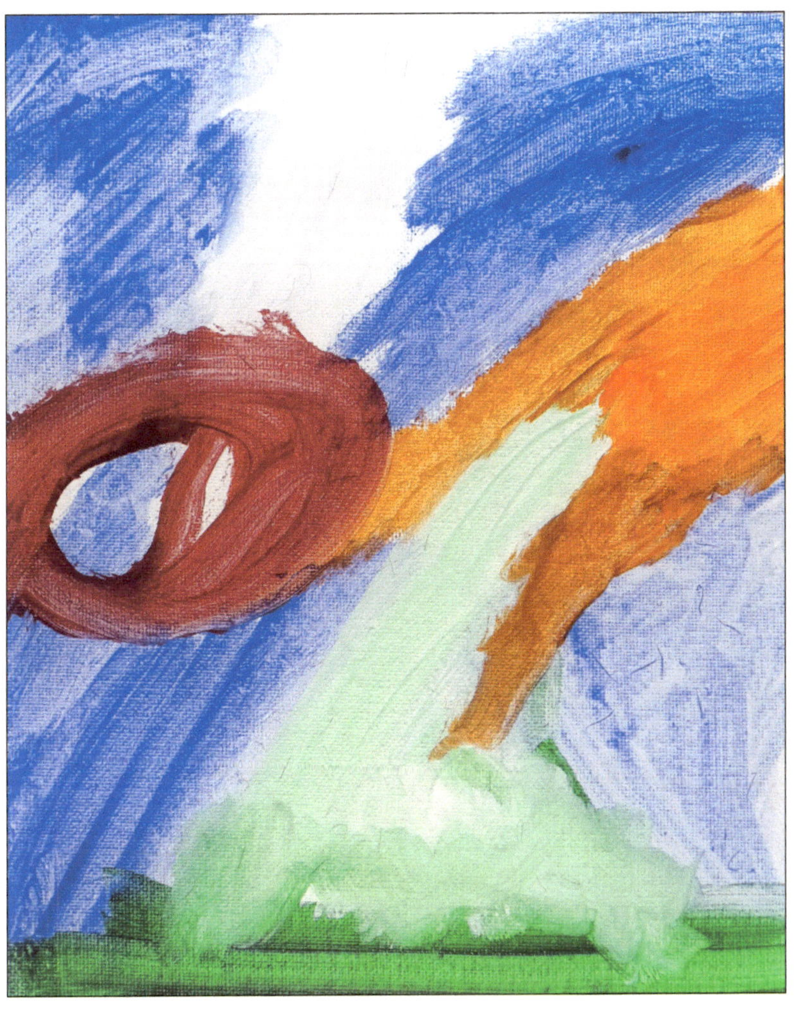

Like over and over—like in
my head
Or is it really more about
this dream?
Like a dream world—inside
and out
And your life—that you had
known before
And running and running
Like in the dark
Or is it really the awakening
twist?

Like up in the sky
And all you see is air
That falls into place
Like the eclipse of the sky
In the field that you're in
And just standing there

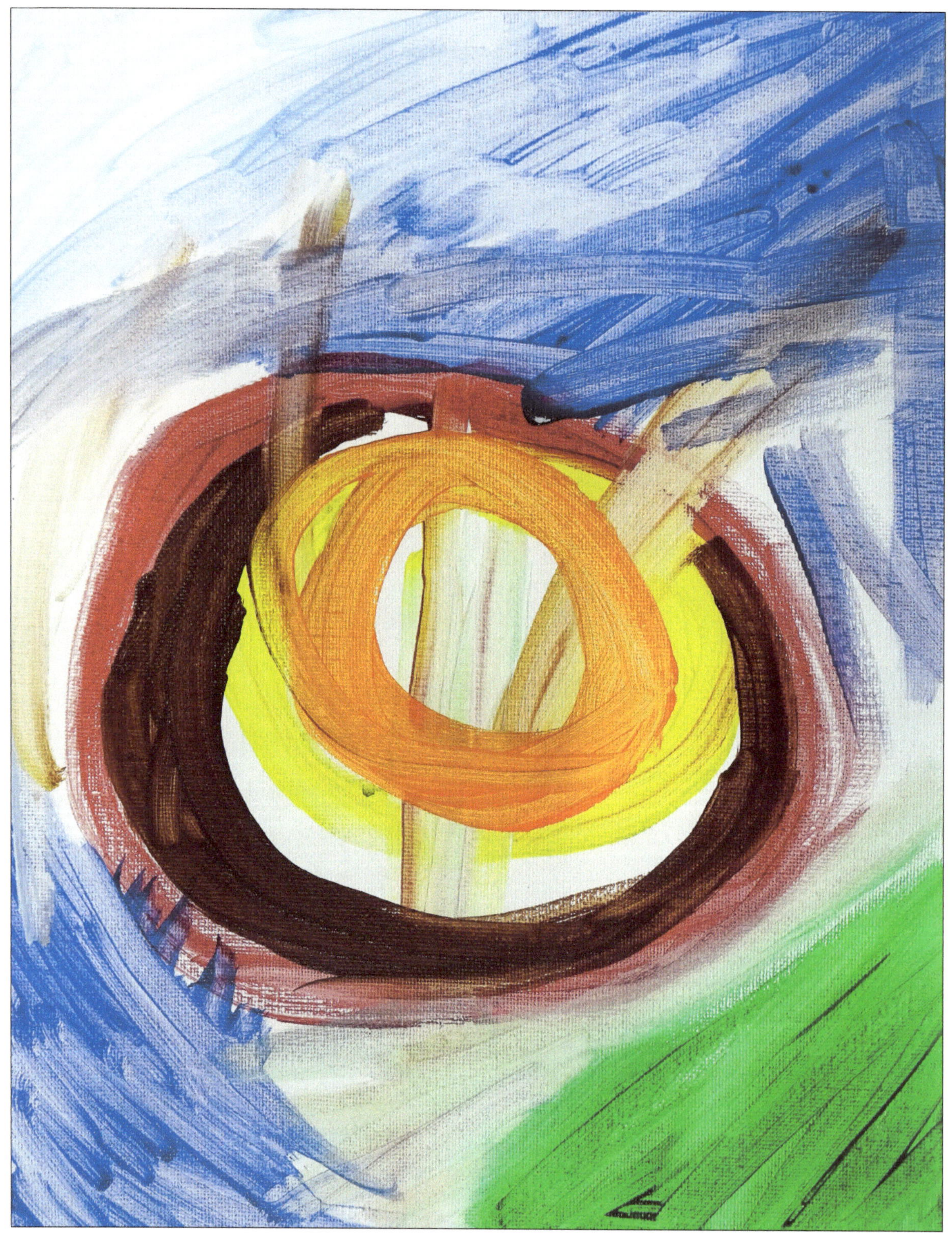

The wandering setting, peacefully
of this circle of beyond—of more
than anything else—of LIFE in itself
and of that more of the epic blue moon
in that dark sky.
And that circling surrounding
and movement of anything in that moment,
or anything else—like it's own disguise—
like a pair of eyes—wandering in the dark,
in the cold darkest—of a dream—
Like you can't remember—or is it really
    a memory?
Like with anything but pretend—
Like shadows—and that wild darkness of life
and more—like the Earth
Like with Spirits—that you never have seen
Like a missing soul—or is it more than anything?
Like my wrath that goes there forever.
Likely—like it's own creation—and with color
but only like this moment in time
that will be discovered but with time.
and it will be
forever

The wandering setting of this dream
of LIFE—as itself... and more than anything,
and beyond. Peacefully, of that big, dark, cold sky.
and more. Like eternity—of the epic—of LIFE,
and how it falls into place. And this moment,
creating itself—than anything of the wild—life,
of SILENCE, or is it really just a dream?
and of this memory—Like
that goes there, forever—but we never
say forever—
OR IS IT KINDA LIKE the future—and
what it means—and it will be discovered,
but with time. Like a circling hole—
and that surrounding that will be remembered,
like the distance—of this blank space, that's pretend.
Because you could never SEE it.
But sometimes
we can hear it. OR is it NOT? But with
movement and this pair of eyes, wandering the
distance—like it's own disguise—like the
wind, moving—but you can't really tell—
or how it feels. Like being ALIVE.

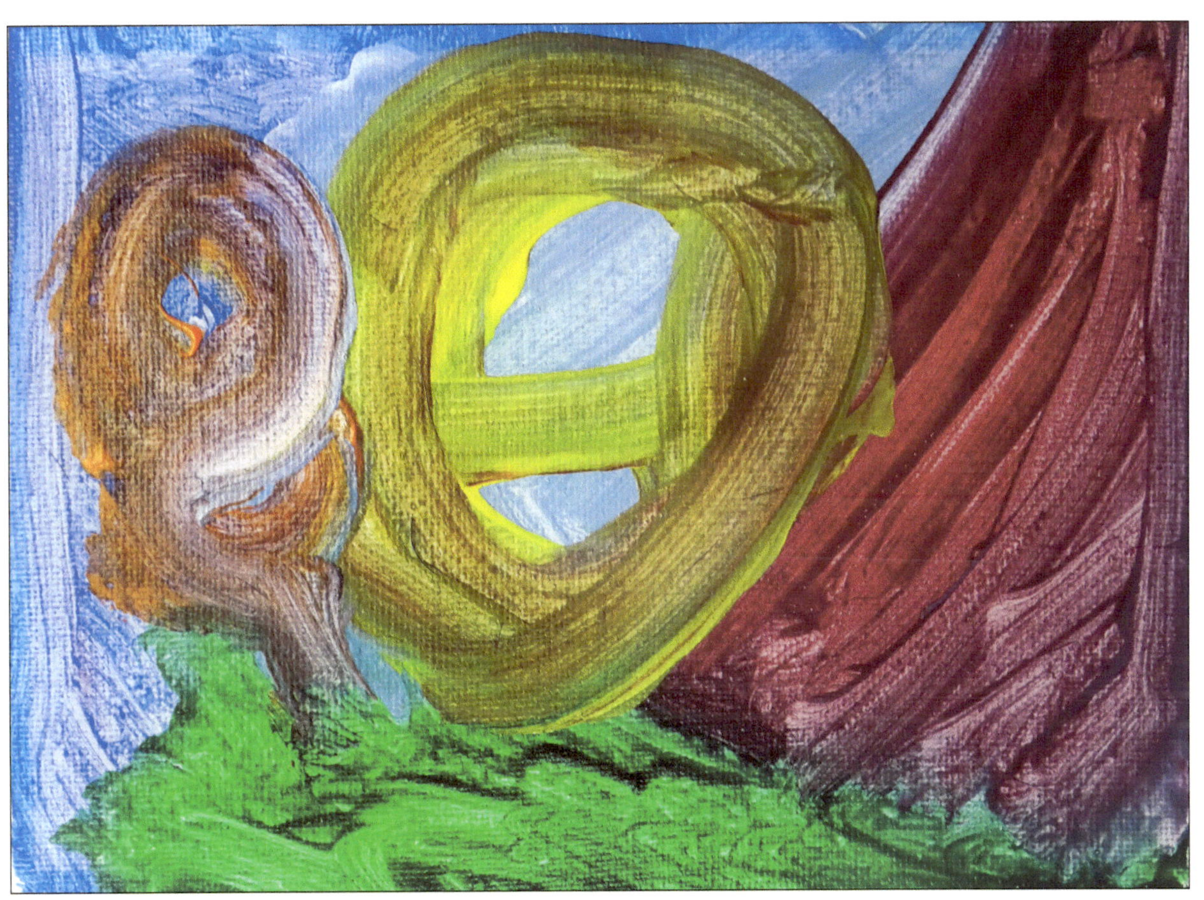

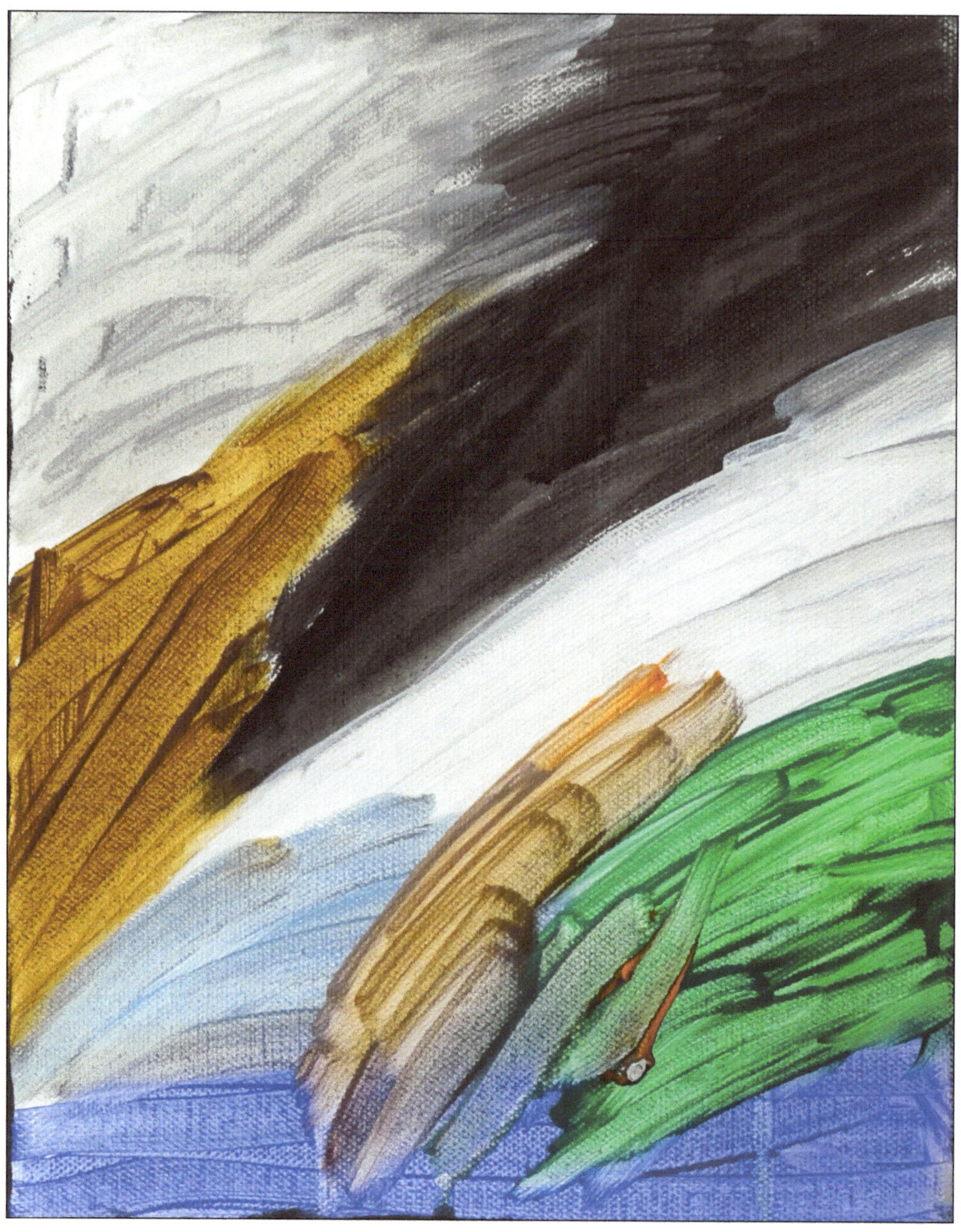

The wandering eyes of life—
An opportunity
of anything, and anyone, and
of each other
And beyond—when you put
your mind to it.

And believing in yourself
And always more.
Like having an idea—and
more to it—
Because this is what I
believe in.

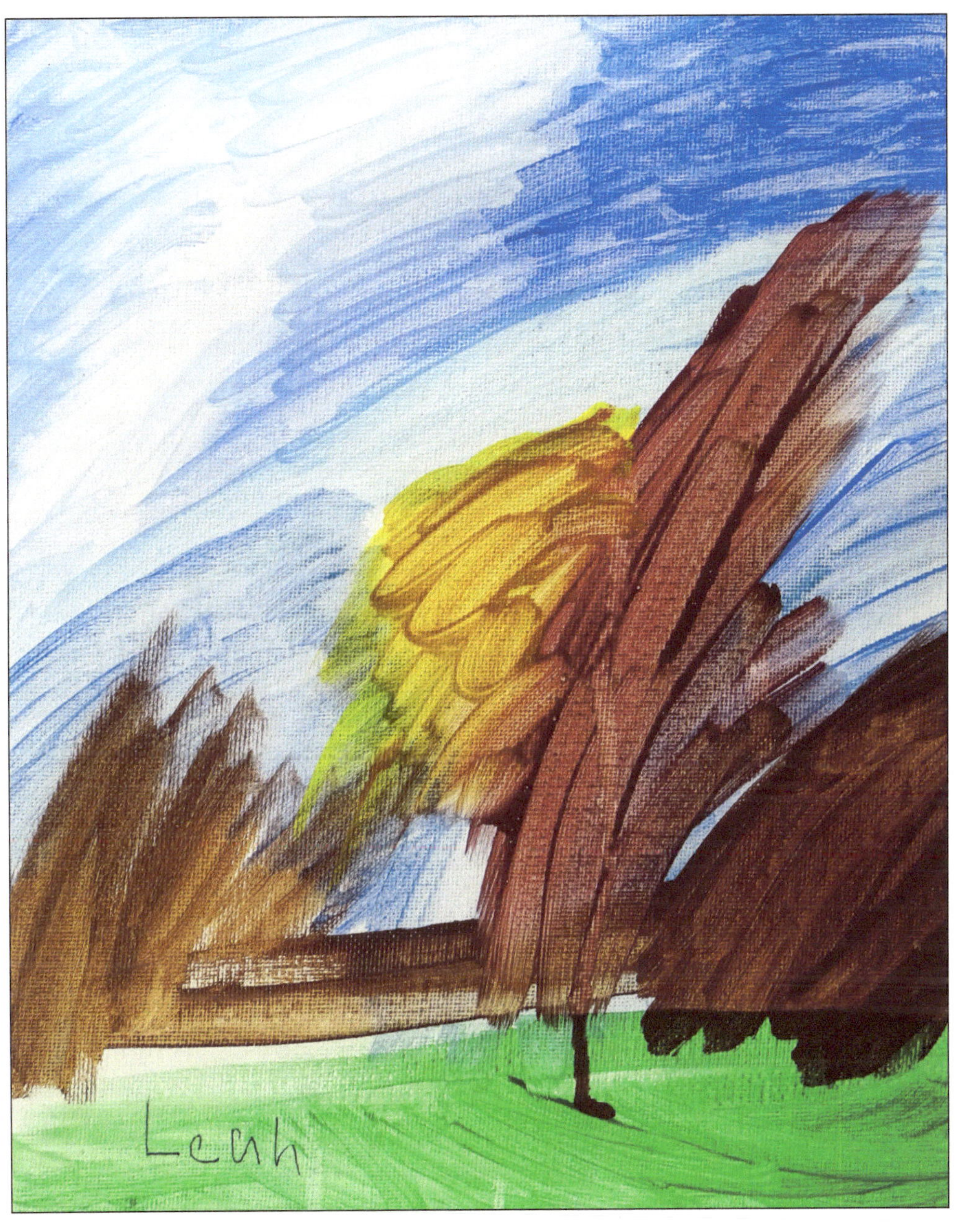

And so much more is
possible—
That you could do it
And keep going forward.
Because that's what life is.
And discovering the
impossible journey,
and creating this next chapter
in this destiny
Through an opening, like
another opening door.

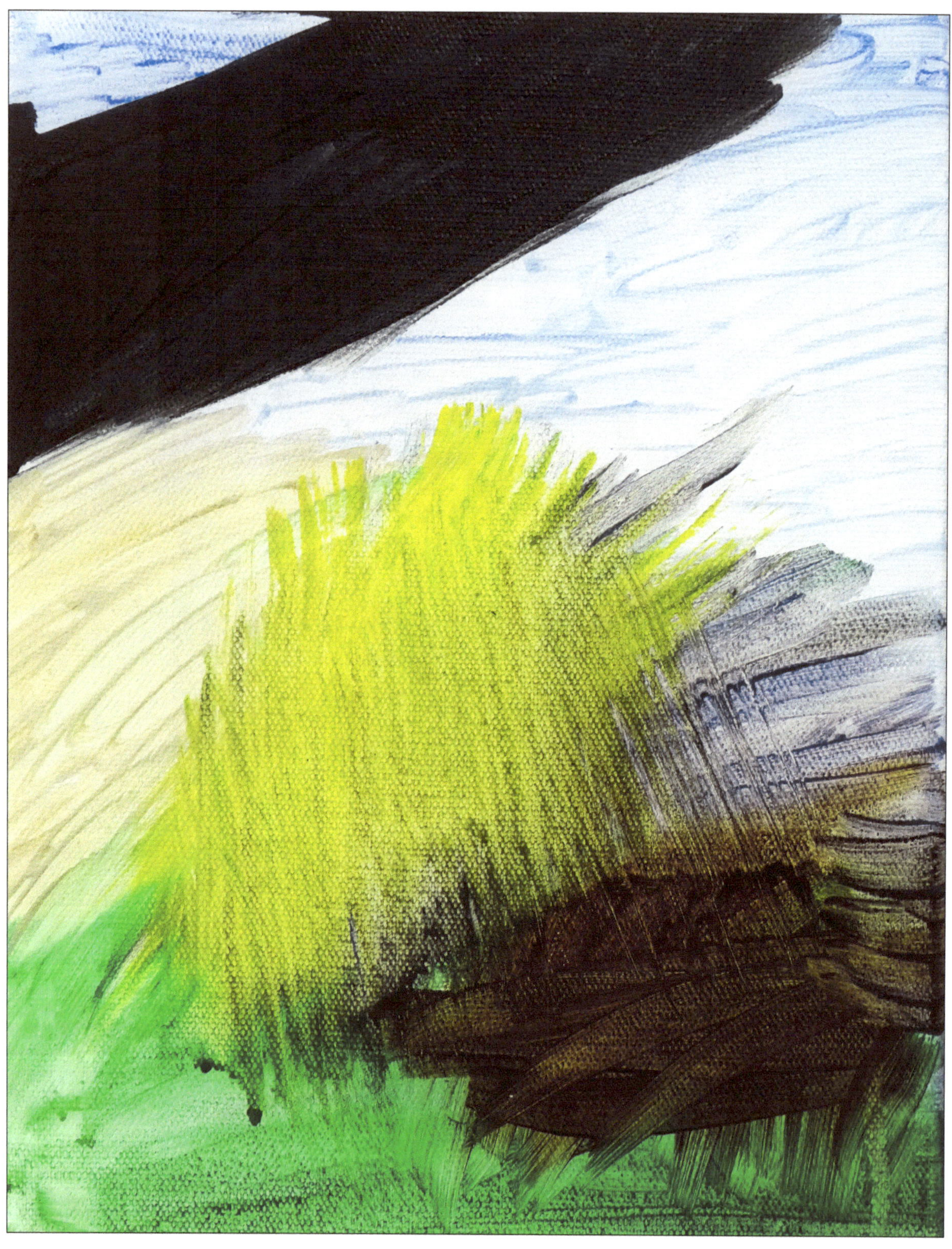

The wandering whispering movement of color
And of this moment in time
Like over and over
Like in this mirror frame of silence
That makes you want to scream
Like within air and out
And more of this chapter piece
Like a movie-scene of life
And being in this
Behind, opening twist
And now, and more than ever
Sometimes in life, and in this magical
That's in the dust
Like the movement of air
That falls into place
And all these colors,
Completely falls and into anything
Like with music
and anything else that comes to it before
It will be noticed, in the future

The mystery wandering distance setting
Of a peacefully dream of silence
And parts of your pair of eyes
Looking through the glass
The whispering wind, inside and out
And before, like it was
And anything
Of a dream of the dark blue moon sky
And falls into place slowly
And the surrounding of the epic, dark hole—
That fades out, mysteriously
And more to it
Like movement of color
Or it is more than anything?
Like this moment in time, like the future
And years before that too
And like this discovery, that will be solved
But with time
And in that life
And many, many years,
Like 200 years—
And, like, here we are now
Of this adventure
Of life in itself
And that is us.

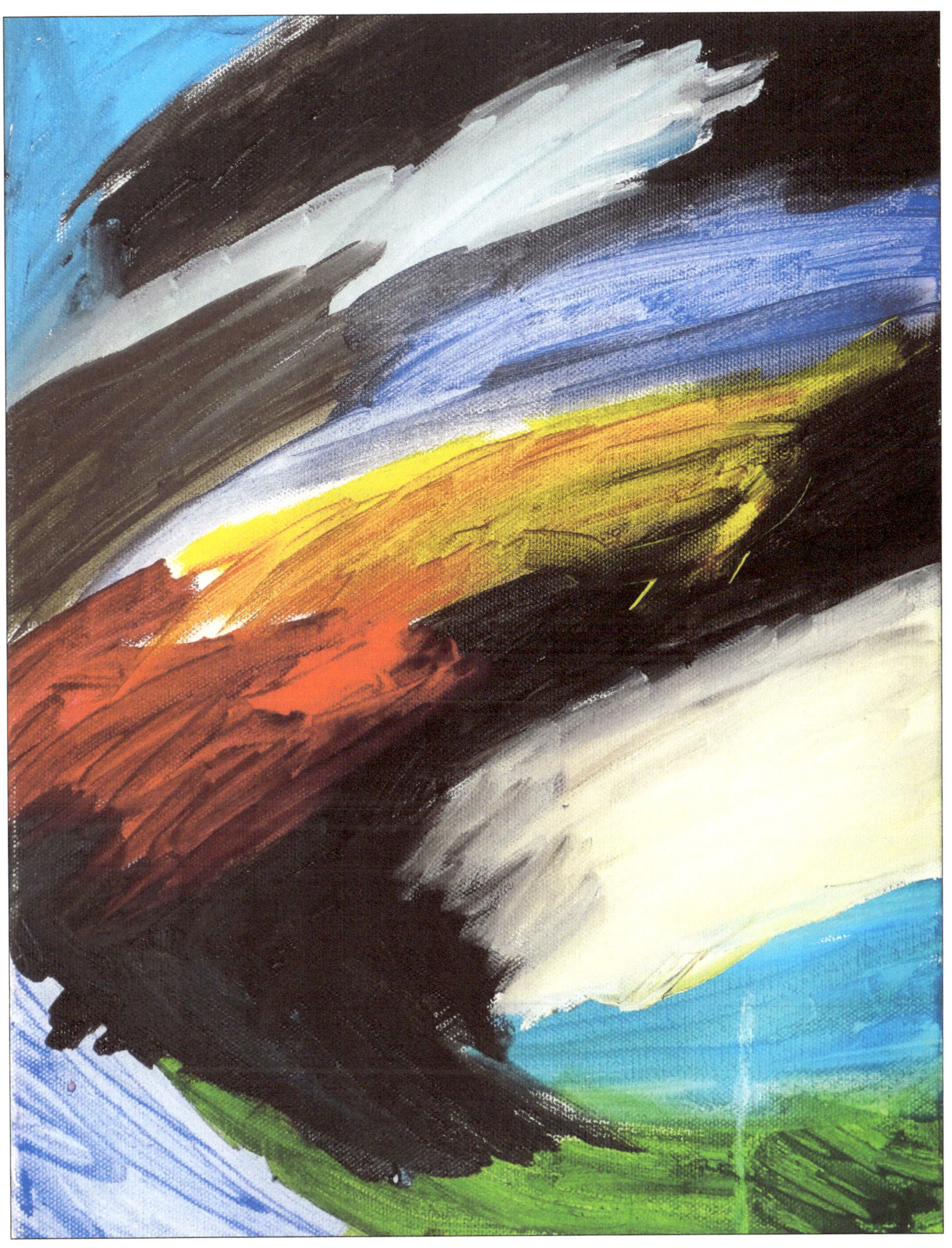

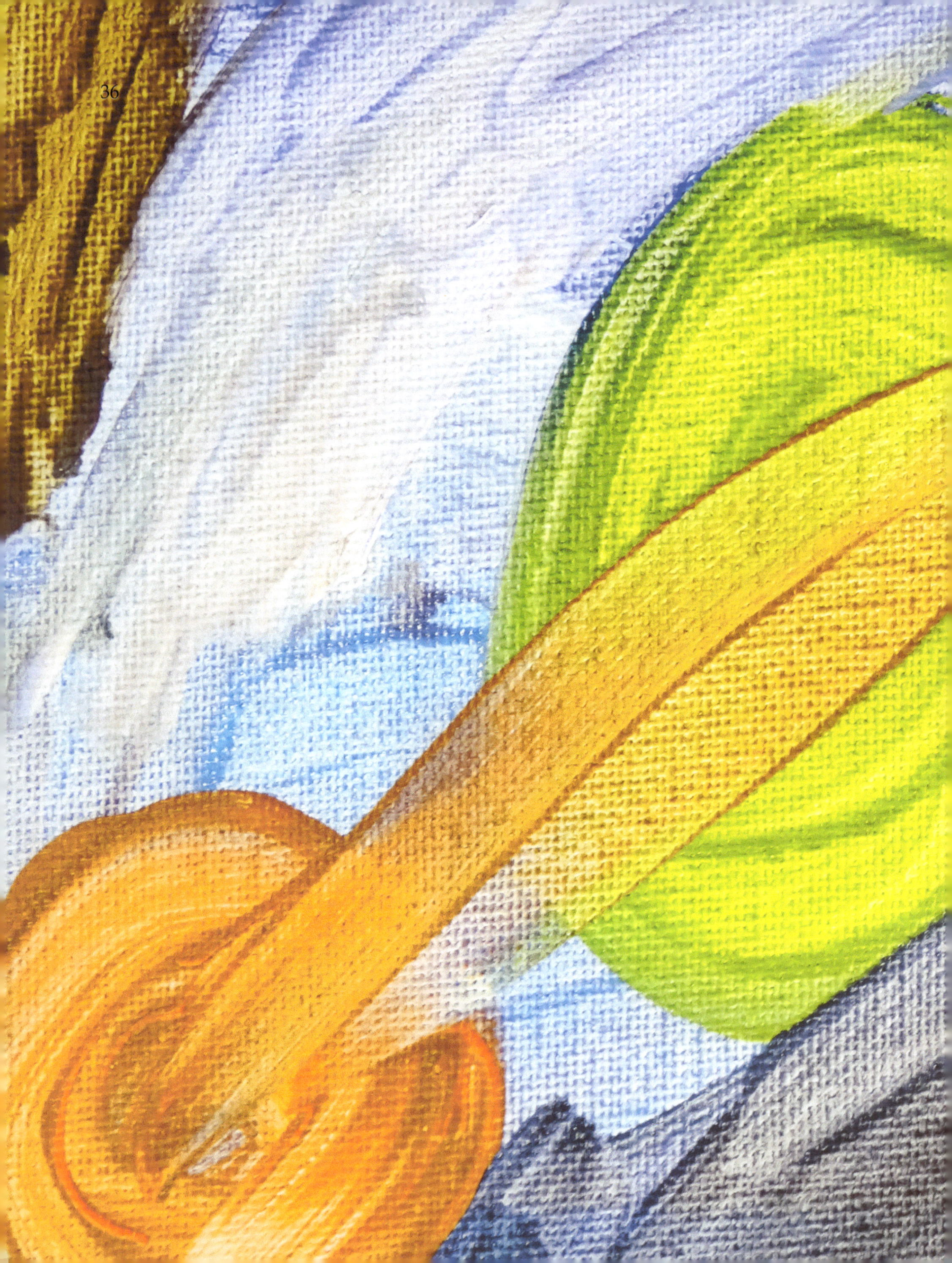

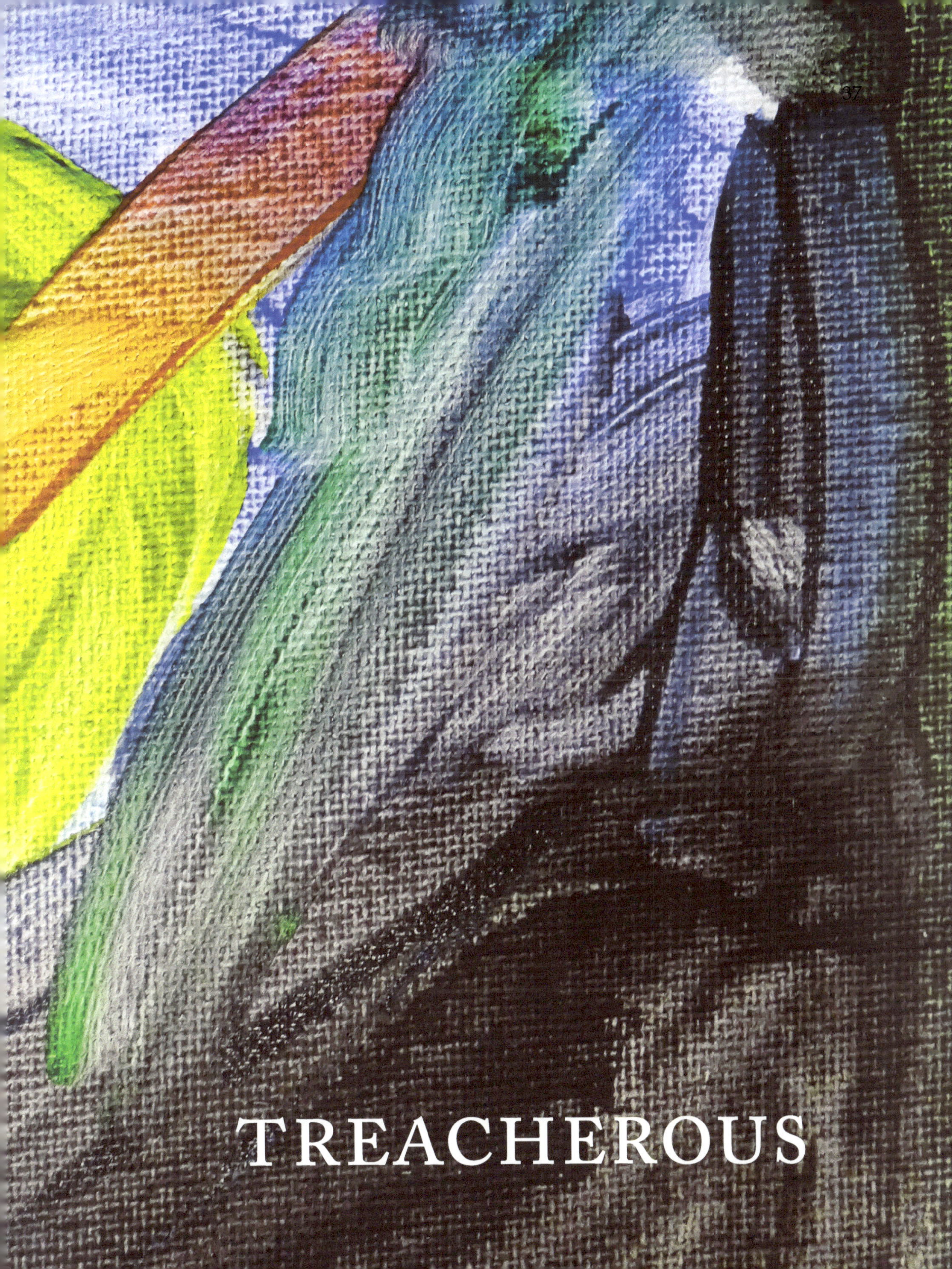

TREACHEROUS

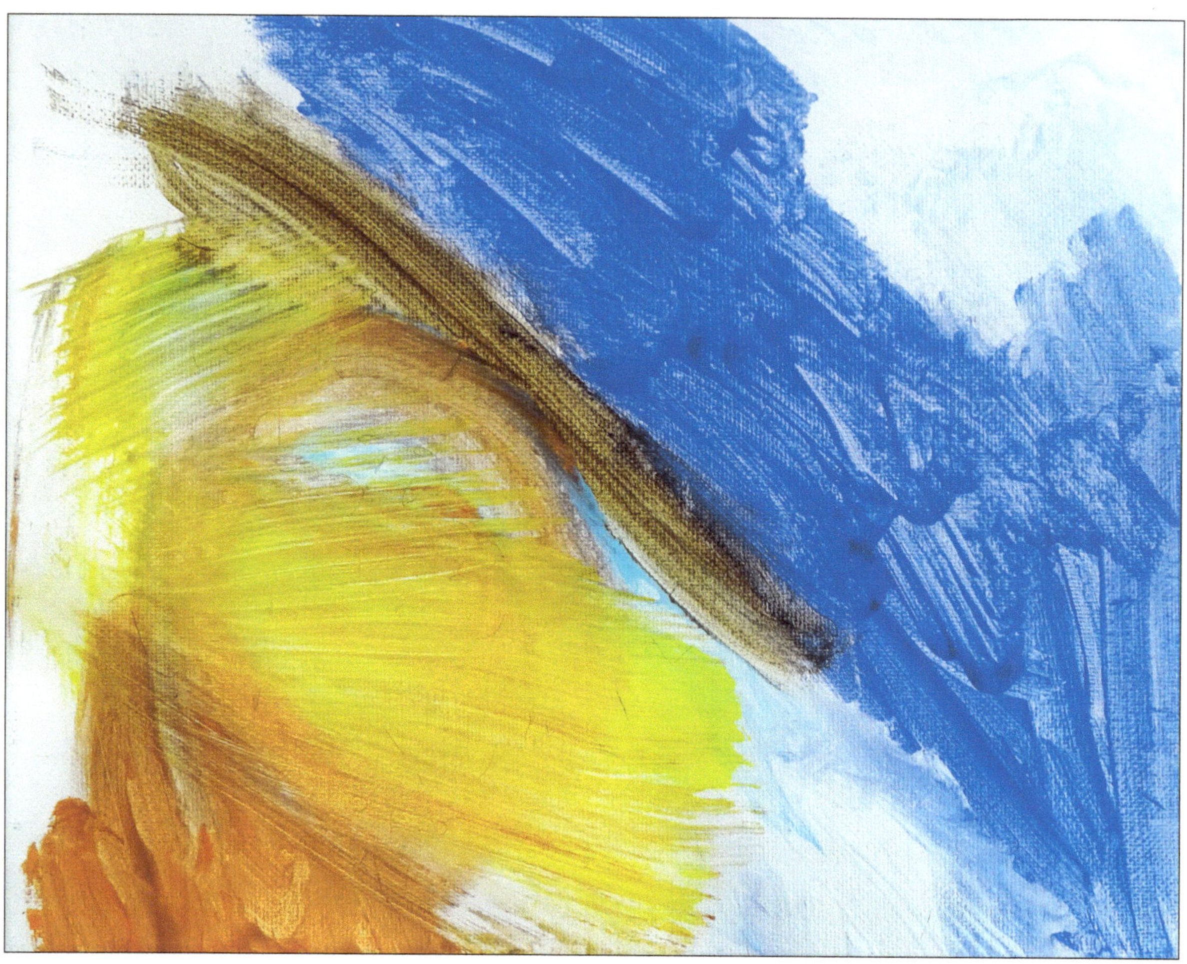

Treacherous Setting

Treacherous setting, peaceful cleansing
inside and out
of the wandering eyes
Cleansing of my glaring spark,
Of pieces and pieces and man, many more
In the dark spiracle of the wandering
eyes that look
through the wandering gates
Like myself that looks back at me
Like a creature in the dark that is so
different but so
mysterious
Of a distance circling that completely
caves in and
into pieces
Like a timeline zone that completely zones
out into place
Of pieces of fantasies, like a mirror frame that
glows back
and into within
An eternity in life and reason, and in itself
like an

awakening twist
Moments in time and wonder,
Like a solver that wonders and creeps out
the wandering
That moves and cleanses into a mirror frame
Out in the world and what it is in itself, like the
wandering eyes
That is so sacred and many, many secrets
that nobody
even knows what it is
Or as itself, that completely fades out like a
mirror frame
that fades out more
Glowingly in the dark of discovering
Because that lost lonely gypsy—that dies—
but she's also
still around forever
Even that she is so different from others—
and many,
many more others around
That fades out of that quest, destiny that
completely
craves into place
And circling and into this discovery of
eternity of
life and reason
In this life that is so meant to be, or not to be
that question
And of these biggest hints of discovery,
and of this
journey concept
This lost lonely gypsy, that is so out there,
That what I meant to say was:
When she dies of her own tears, she cries
of glory
Horror whispering in the dark of a nightmare
that cleanse
even more
Of a dream that is still there for centuries
And many, many years that have gone by
And of myself, in my eyes I'm still asleep and
in myself
Like this destiny that craves into a journey
And shadows that cleanse into a lost, lone gypsy
Her spirit that whispers in the nightmare, in
the rough, in
the dark
And of eternity of life, and in itself of reason,
and reason
enough
That completely has meant to be, or not to
be that
question
And the goodness of herself and her glowing
heart
Filled with gold, so magical within and
in herself
That glory, beyond and within
The heart that never breaks

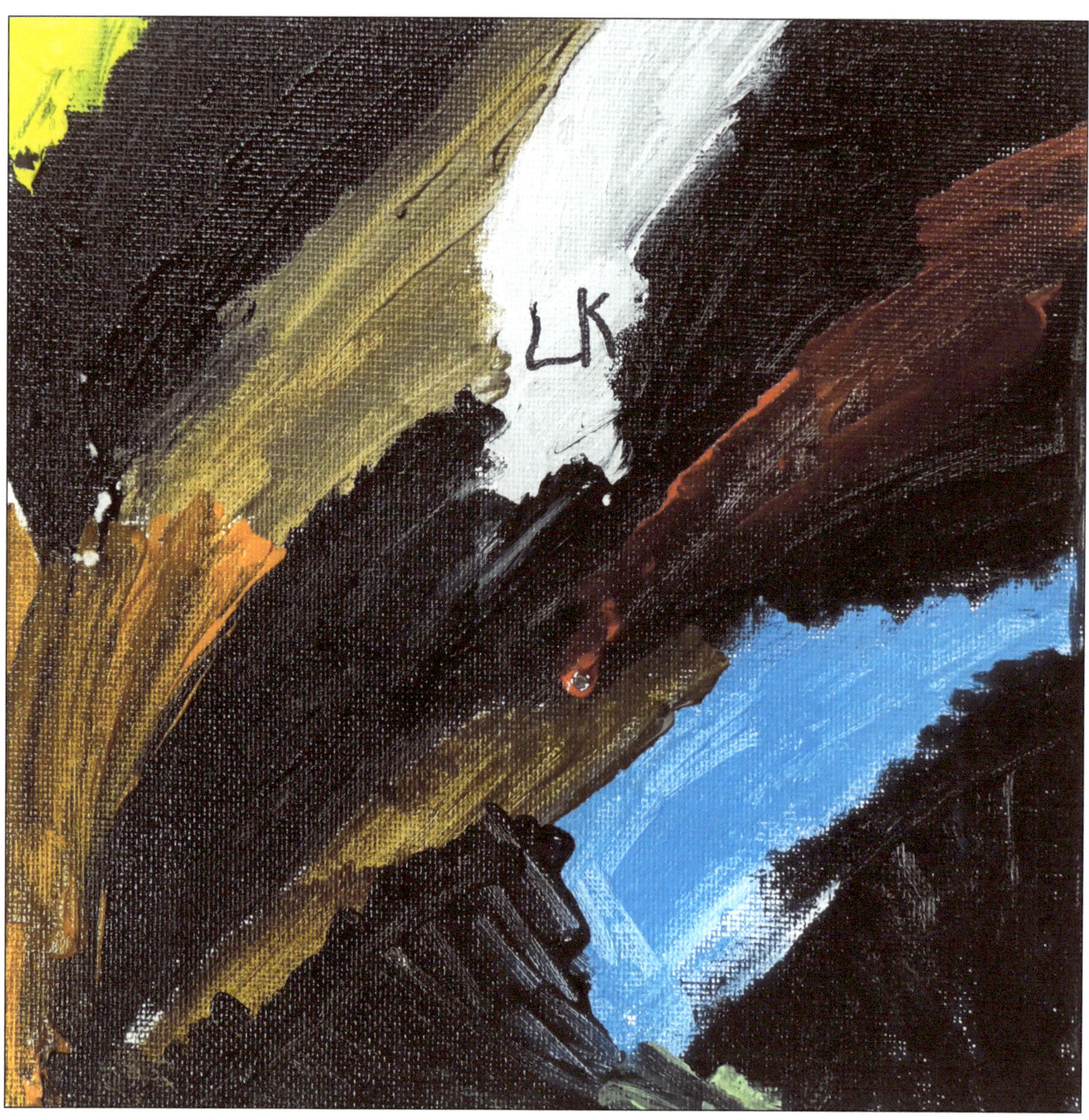

Treacherous setting peacefully
Silent night of dreams whispering out of this fantasy imagery
Of that night—like the dead of air
That we could never hear,
But it feels like it IS

Even when that is disappearing forever
Even more than anything, like going back behind
That we see, of that life—
That we have never known before
Then later, of that hour—in that time

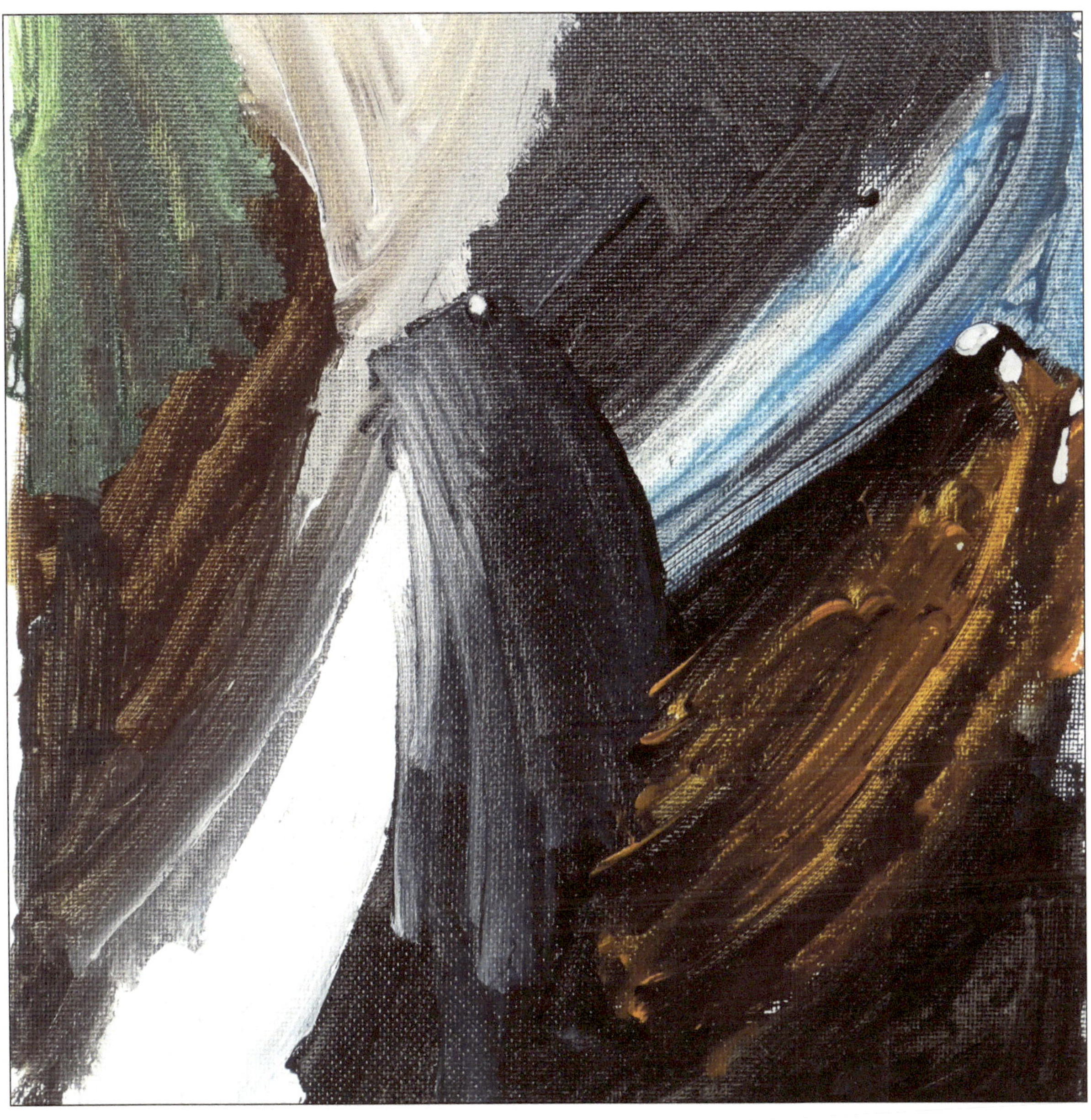

Of that night—
I look at the sky from my window
Even when I'm just like my painting—
That I see, that I have done forever
The rain falls out
Even more—within and without
Behind those years
Like shadows—that you could never see

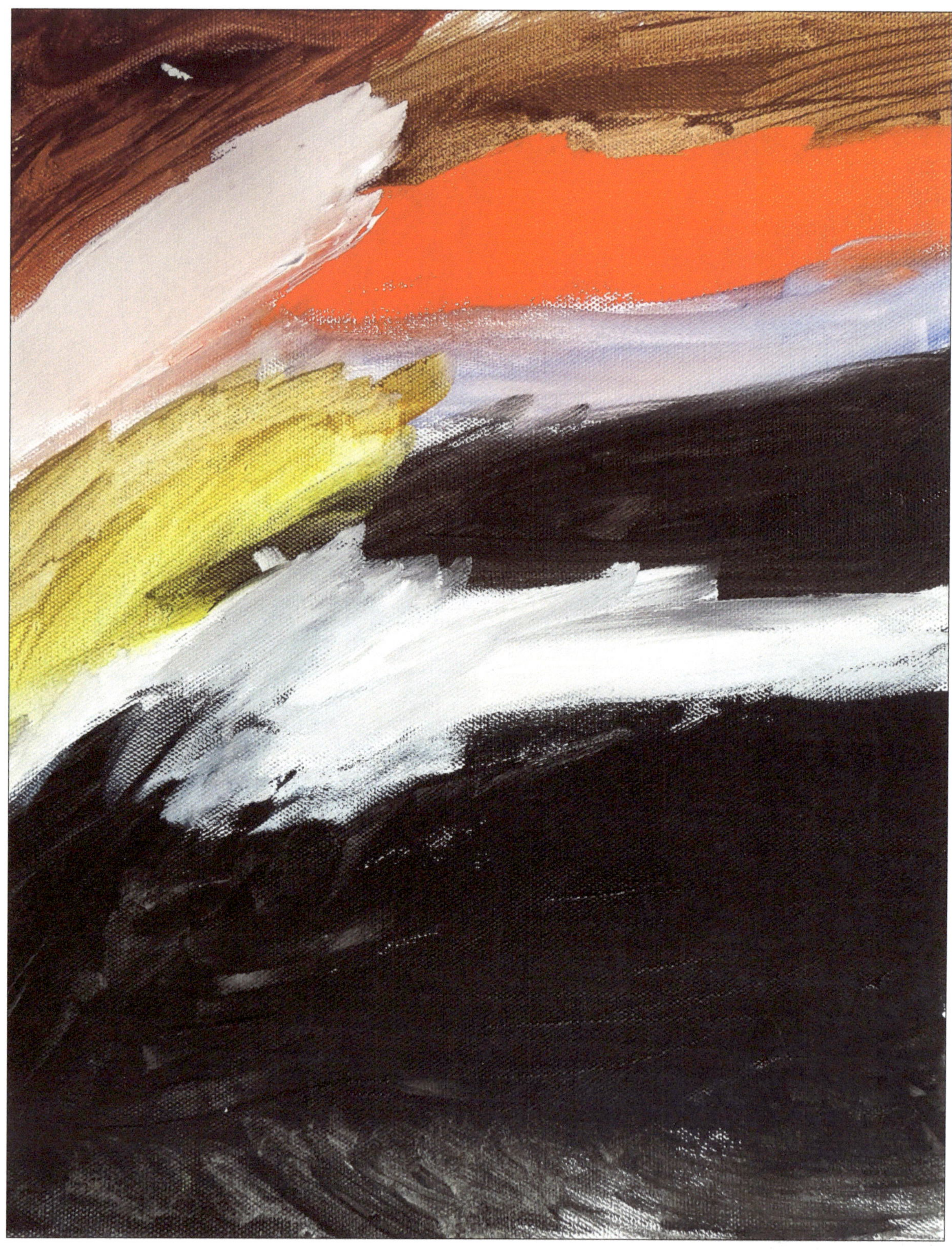

Broken Mirror

Like a broken mirror frame
But what is in that frame?
Because it's not really there, real.
A ghost of my spirit and in this soul
I know it's not there
People around us, that are so committed
to themselves
But us people, our people, we matter the most
Like pictures and pictures inside my head,
with words
But it's not really pictures inside of my head
Just words:
ticking and ticking
Of life in there, in itself: treacherous wonder
Desires of life and treasure
Of treacherous
and discovering life in itself and without.
Fading, crystalling out of air.
Hanging like a piece of thread
Like beginning in time—of moments in time,
in life
With others that are so different—
These souls are nothing
But what is really of souls, what is a soul?
That they have inside
People that are so different, so alike; that's us
In the life of darkness, watching and watching
all those other people.
Face to face, in my life, with nothing inside
with fading out

Treacherous Wonder

Treacherous moments in time of wonder,
Spiracle of life in itself fading, fading out inside of my present.
Piece by piece, over and over of the distance of life,
In the dark of silence.
Craving and craving galaxy in the dark
Spiracle dark inside of myself within, without nothing inside, fading.
My breathe taken and taking in that time of wonder,
And in that dark of wisdom
In souls reaching and reaching out of others
Not caring, but in that life of darkness, of secrets within.
Like the movement of the wind, to a next opening door
Awakening of life itself and inside anything at all.

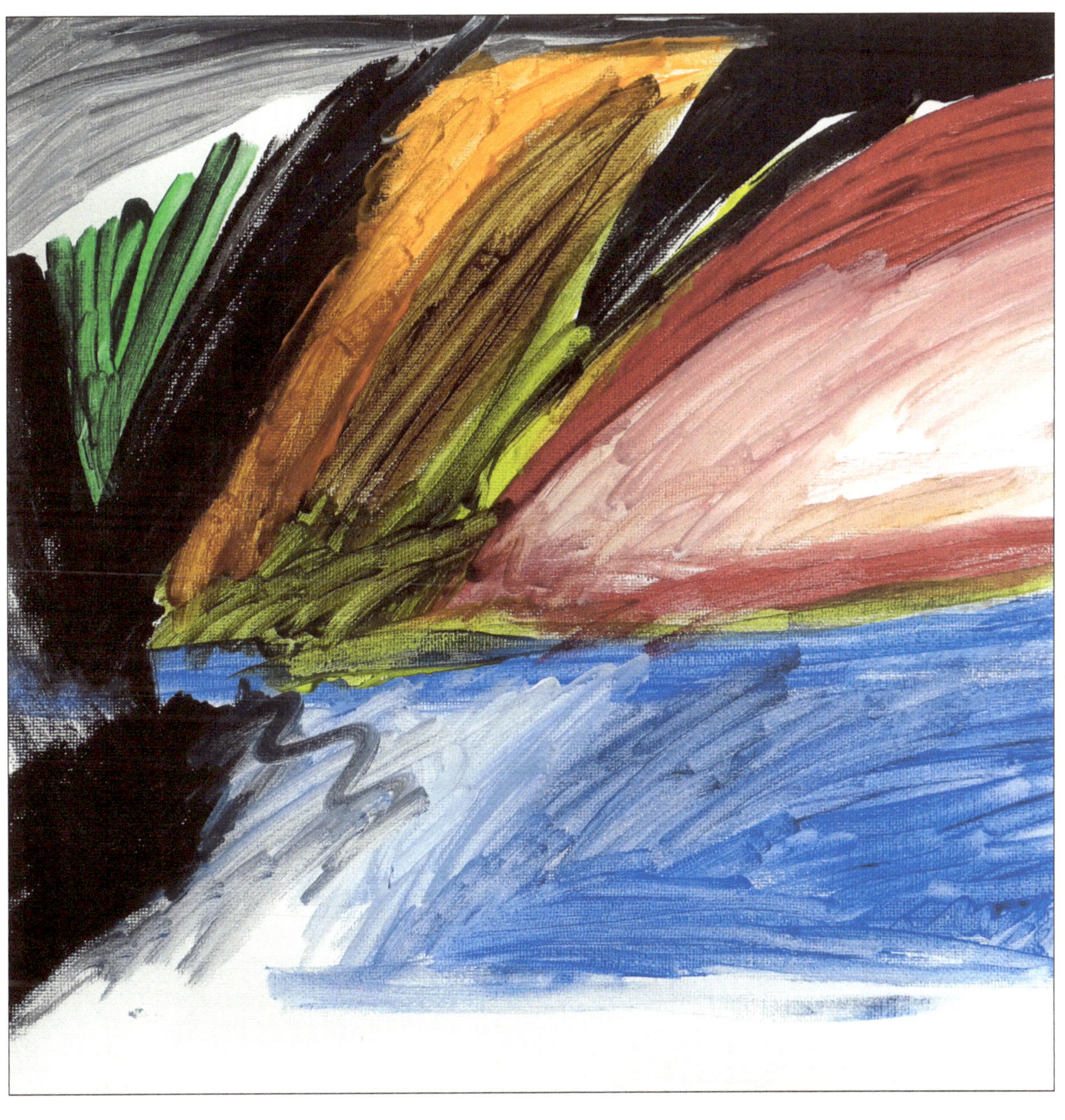

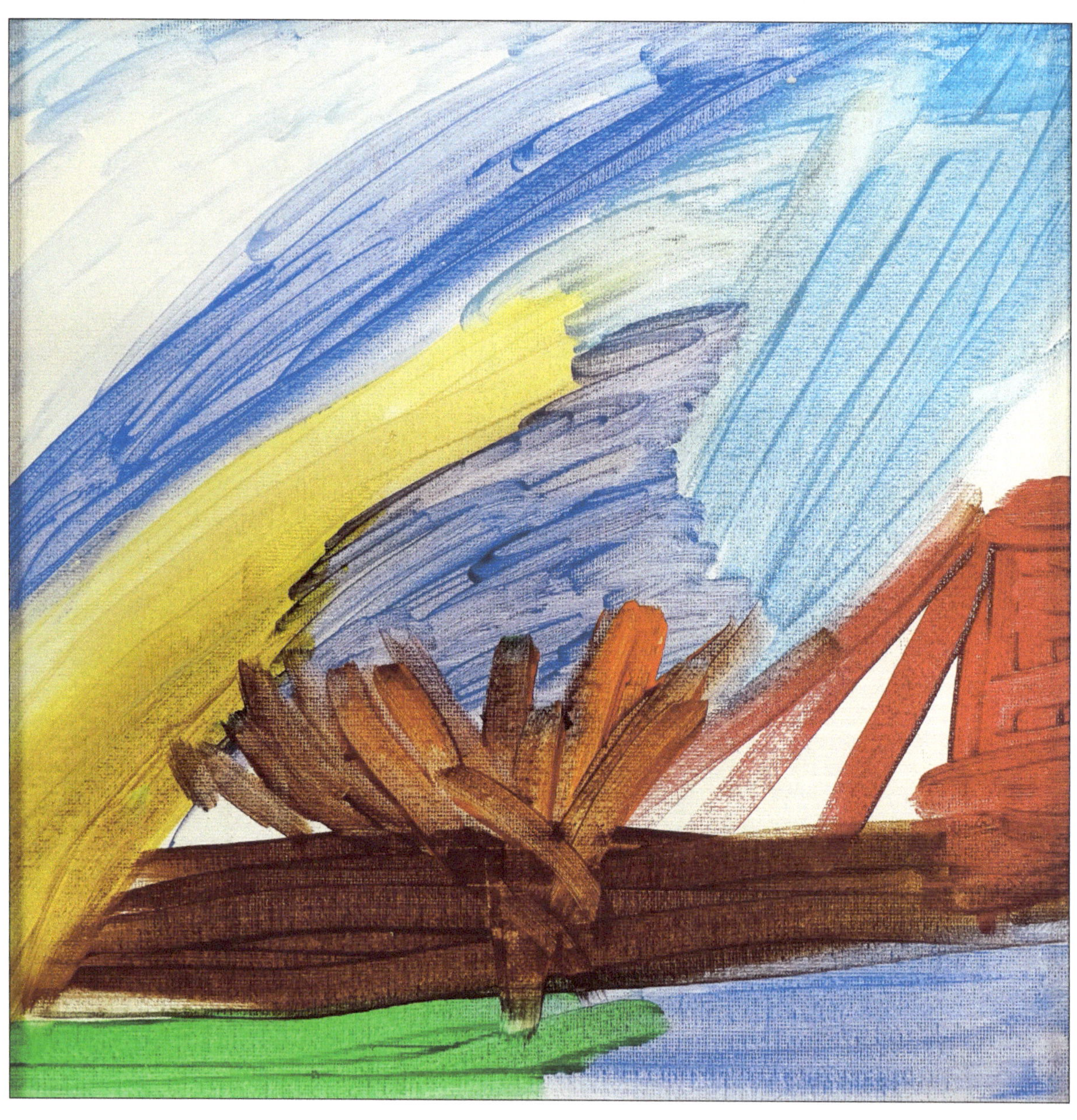

Treacherous Setting—

Lightning rod of the surface of wonder
A cross between the lines, like a piece of
drawing in itself,
Within, without,
Without reach within
The distance between sacred lighting in the dark
Crossroad in the dark, in time of wonder, in
life, in itself
Fading and fading without
Drawing back inside and out,
Like hanging out and pulling backwards in
this cold, stone wall.
In the dark, until death and life,
Like this wall of silence
Over and over, like a piece of a lightning rod
Treacherous piece of a chapter
Breaking and breaking, peacefully craving
destiny
Through the air, underneath myself
Fading and drawing out
Unwrapped of my soul, deeply
"try to break me" you say?
Never going to happen.
In life and sacred destiny, historically of myself
Piece by piece, in life as we know it
It's never going to change
But in life, in the world of deepness,
Of many, many more people in the world that
I see
So filled—of life, fading and fading like a
piece of a craving
Of destiny like a dream
Of silence in the dust—completely in itself
In the dark of movement, over and over.
Airing through the wall of nothing
Nothing inside of this galaxy
Through the dark—the silent dark of
shadows, of fantasies
Through inside and out, deeply
Desires of awakening—
Opening filled with this broken,
Completely broken heart—entirely ripped out
from inside my soul
So, this story, what I'm saying right now,
right here
Now is the time for this next chapter
Of an opening door
Inside of that door is nothing,
Twisted across the surface of life, discovery
of life
I see this more and more every day of my life
When I'm on this journey
I think that we should bring out a new
beginning to the End.
But I know what's going to happen,
Or what possibly what's going to happen
It's time to fix this
Drawing back to back—of more people to help
And solve this quest—
Treasure for all of us!
That's why we are here,
And we are not going away.

Treacherous piece of a chapter
Breaking and breaking, peacefully craving
destiny
Through the air, underneath myself
Fading and drawing out
Unwrapped of my soul, deeply
'try to break me," you say?
Never going to happen.
In life and sacred destiny, historically of myself
Piece by piece, so possible in life as we know it
It's never going to change
But in life, in the world of deepness,
Of many, many more people in the world that
I see
So filled—of life, fading and fading like a
piece of craving
Of destiny like a dream
Of silence in the dust—completely in itself
In the darkness of movement, over and over.
Airing through the wall of nothing
Nothing inside of this galaxy
Through the dark—the silent dark of
shadows, of fantasies
Through inside and out, deeply
Desires of awakening—
Opening filled with this broken,
Completely broken heart—entirely ripped out
from inside my soul
So, this story, what I'm saying, right now,
right here
Now is the time for this next chapter
Of an opening door
Inside of that door is nothing,
Twisted across the surface of life, discovery
of life
I see this more and more every day of my life
When I'm on this journey
I think that we should bring out a new
beginning to the End.
But I know what's going to happen,
Or what possibly what's going to happen
It's time to fix this
Drawing back to back—of more people to help
And solve this quest—
Treasure for all of us!
That's why we are here,
And we are not going away.

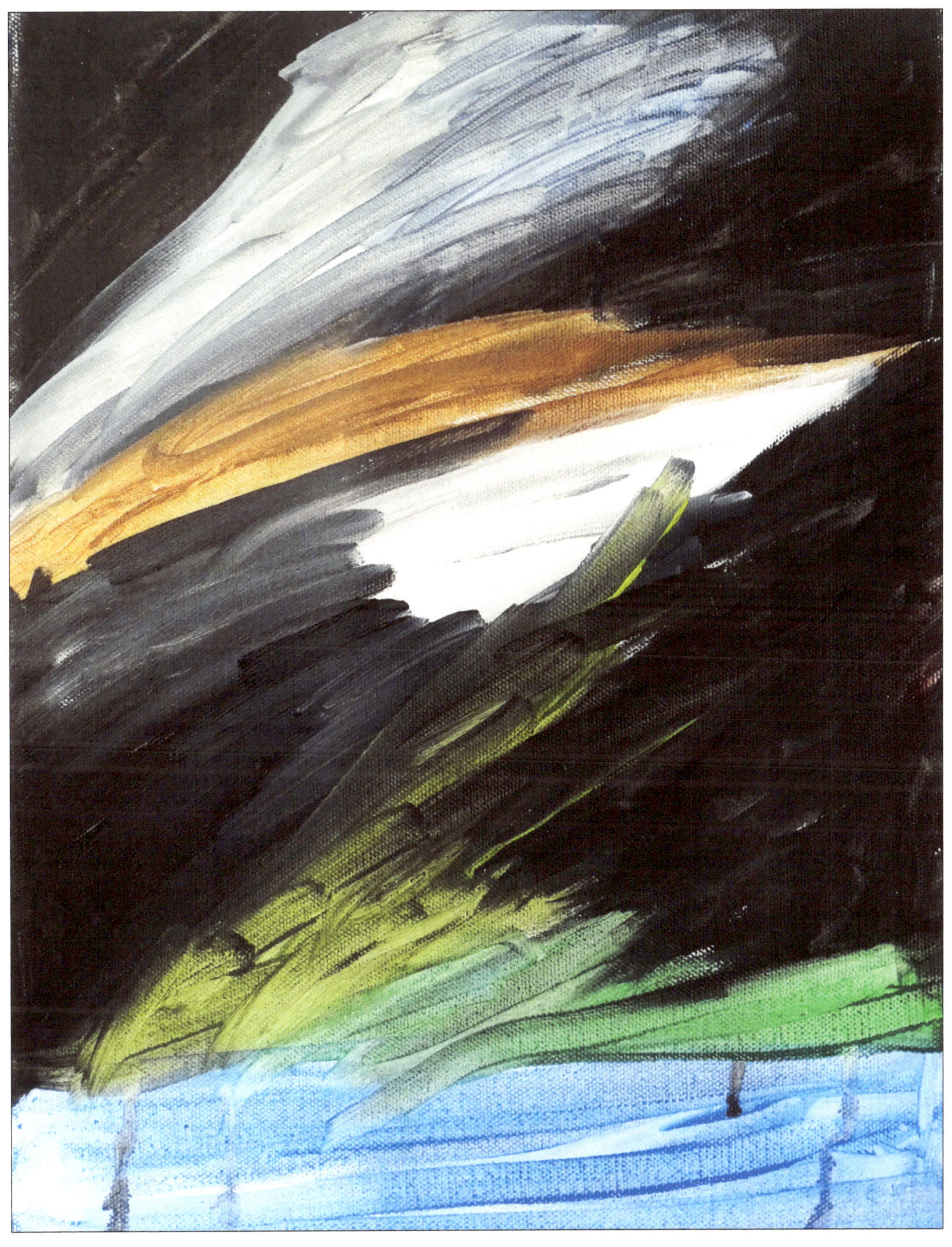

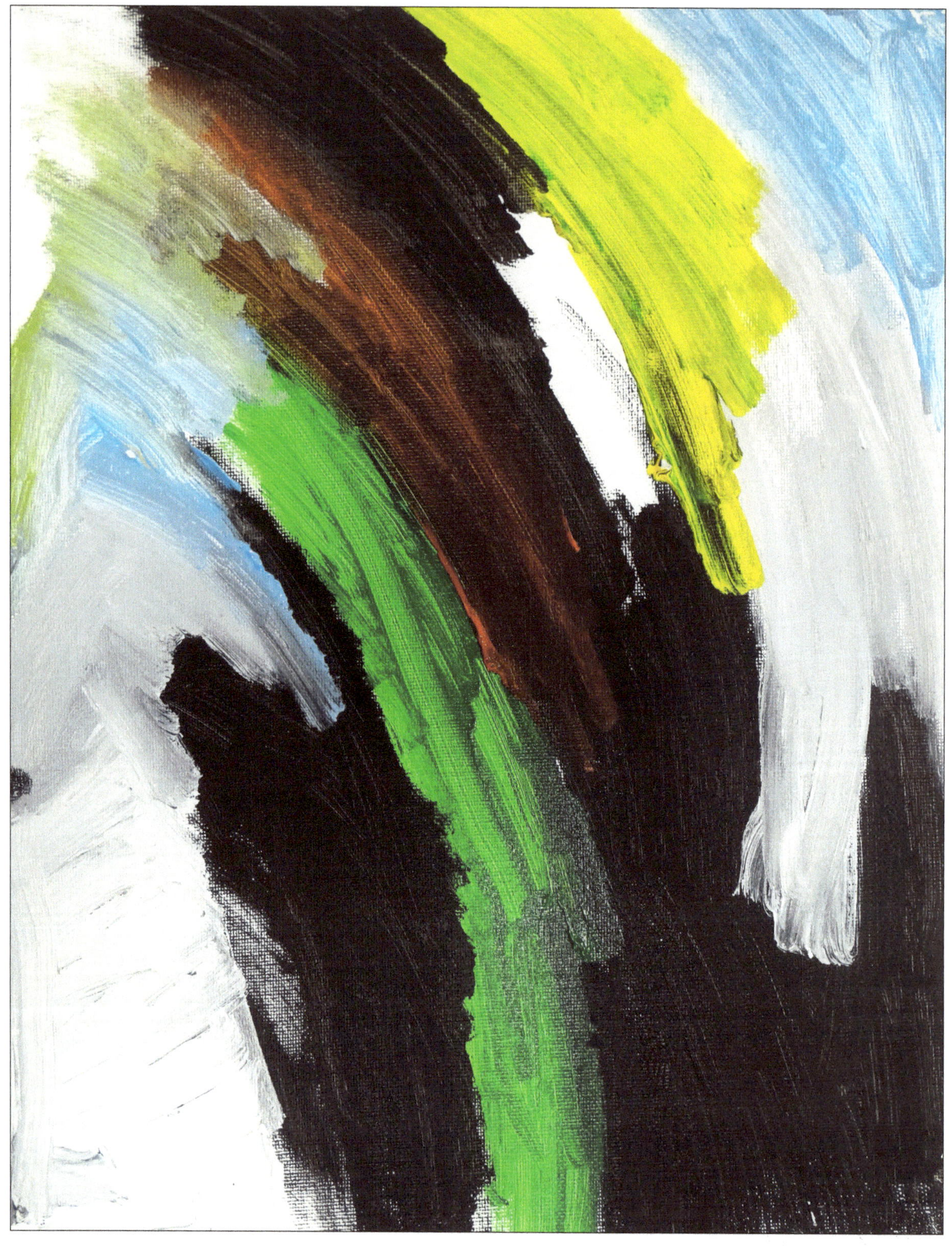

Treacherous setting,
cynical life, of wonder—censoring through
and through the distance—like a piece of
a part twist—
compared of magic, of teardrops falling &
falling out—within and without, without
reach of life—
so apart from us,
like another sentence—
twist through and through—
the shady bird, a raven—
so dark, so there, so not there—
In that time of moments—
like moments of time creeping out like a
shadowy tear,
glass breaking & breaking in the dark of silence
like an awakening—
An opening, back-to-back, shutting back
like a cold, stone wall—through the next
destiny—inside and out,
of tear—falling journey, and of life—in this
life, censoring the quest in the dark
of nothing,
so everything—
like a wandering discoverer out West
like this walking—walking through the
distance—
what is this footstep I'm hearing?
Could be just nothing,
could be anything,
or could it be something else? Like a
wilderness creature in the dark—
so filled apart from us—
is more like outside of us—
like a dirty street in the dark—
like hundreds of millions of things creeping
out in the dark—
like a mystery distance—

Treacherous setting, peacefully shadowing
Shadows of dreams, and this moment in time
Like the sound of the wind in the air of nothing
Of that dead of night
Of silence
Of the crystal-y moon that disappears forever
And more of behind
Like a scene—a present
Of a face—like a mirror frame reflecting
Like a million pieces that scatter
But more than this life—
Of this disguise, creature—
That has never been anything
Of that scene, or unheard
Of this little, sacred, secret town—
That everyone lives in
Kind of like, of this screen—
that you never really see, until it burns out
Like in the dust,
That you will never really recognize
Even years beyond that, and more—
Even within and without
Out from the surface of imagery,
And that time,
That you never expected.

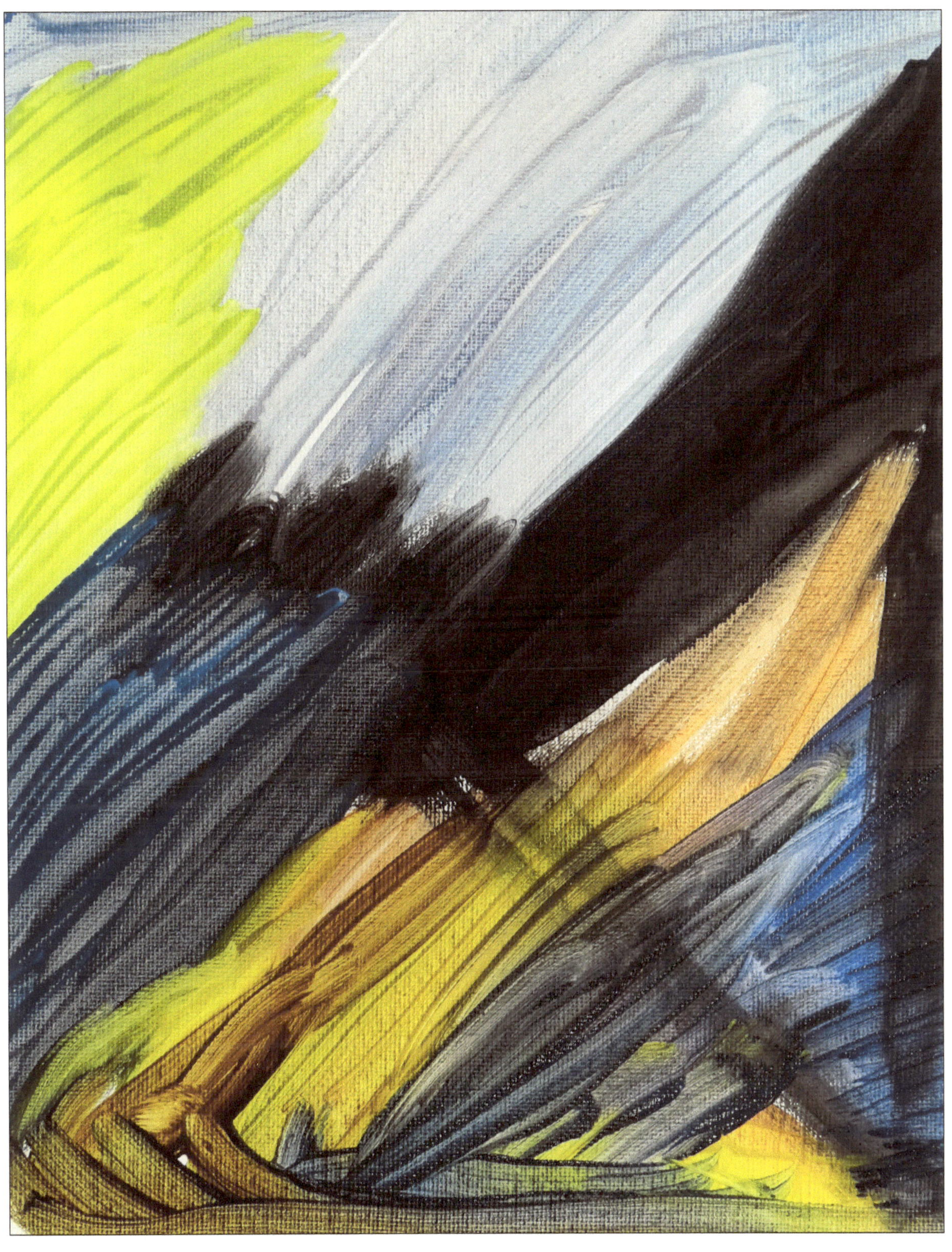

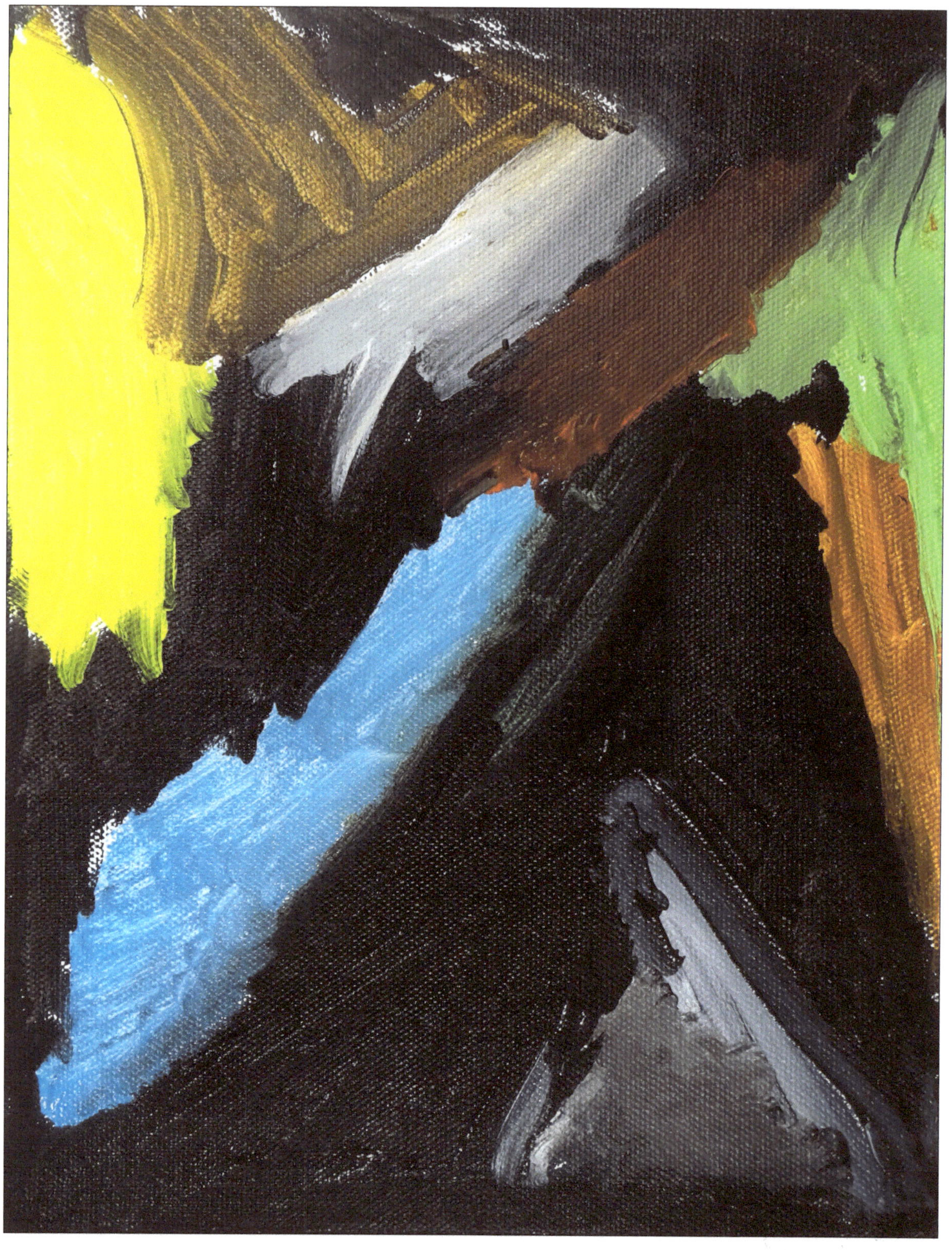

Treacherous setting—
Peacefully dreams of this—
Shadowing souls,
And more of this complex nightmare—
Of the night
Of the midnight twist.
Like a memory,
that's never been solved.
Of eternity, and life—as a sacrifice
Sacrifice of solving,
Anything that you can make out of—
Like a fantasy,
that's recreating itself, and more—
And years beyond, forever.
Even behind everything,
Or anything else that we could find—
And of ourselves—being, continuing,
Even behind, of the end, of a mystery
A burning, whispering diary—
that's never been found.
Of history,
And that's so meant to be,
Or not to be that question...
Like a question of 'more'
Like a reason,
Like a pair of hearts.
And that will be enough of that question,
Of my wrath.

Treacherous setting
Peacefully, of this moment in time—
Out from the distance of the dark
Just like the dead of night creates itself—
    and more,
Within and without—
Of a fantasy dream of imagery—
That anyone, or anybody could see
Like behind of this silver, glare glass
Reflecting of a scene of a pair of eyes
Like a thing,
that's like a creature—in the dark,
In the dead of night,
that is awakening—
That wakes up from everything.

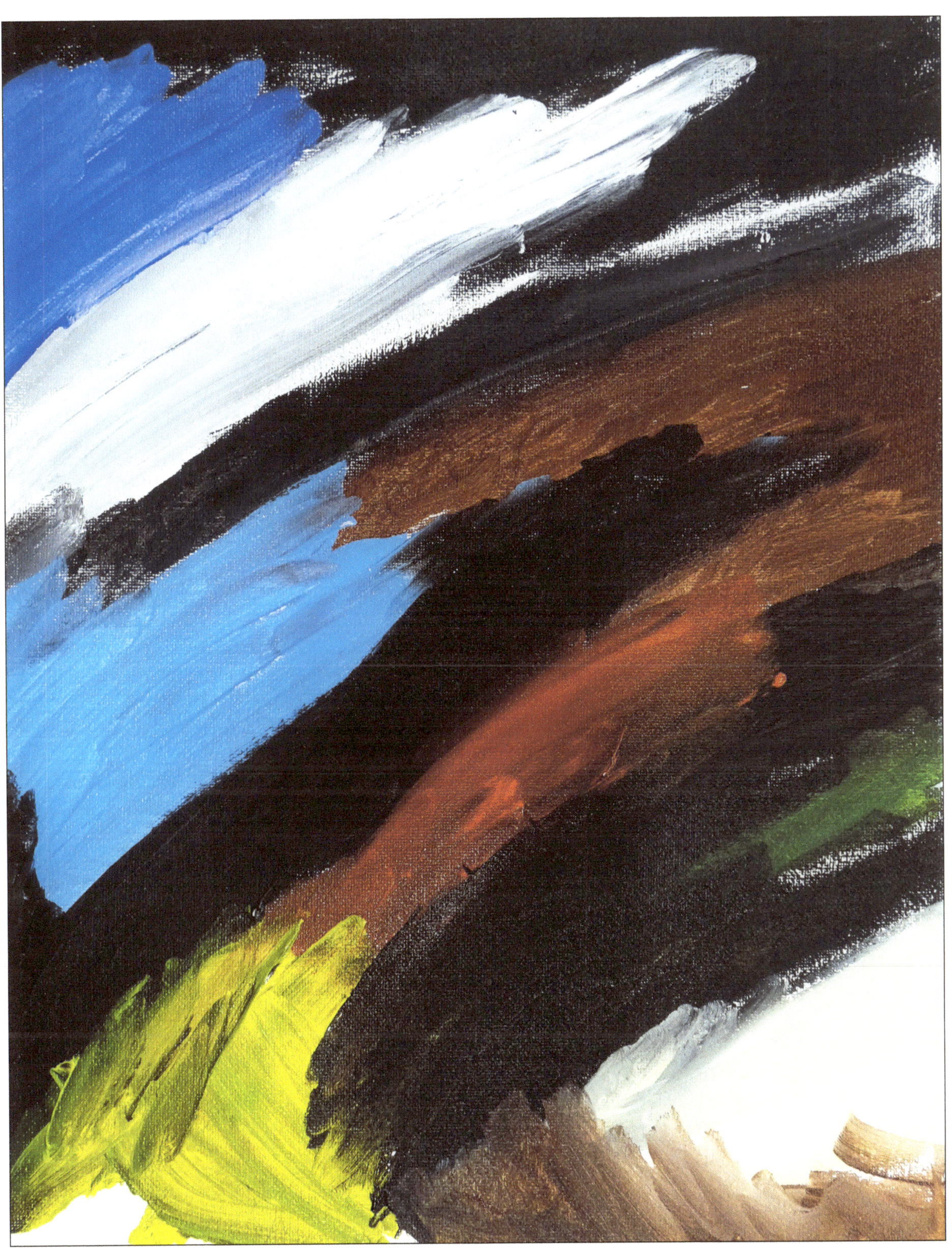

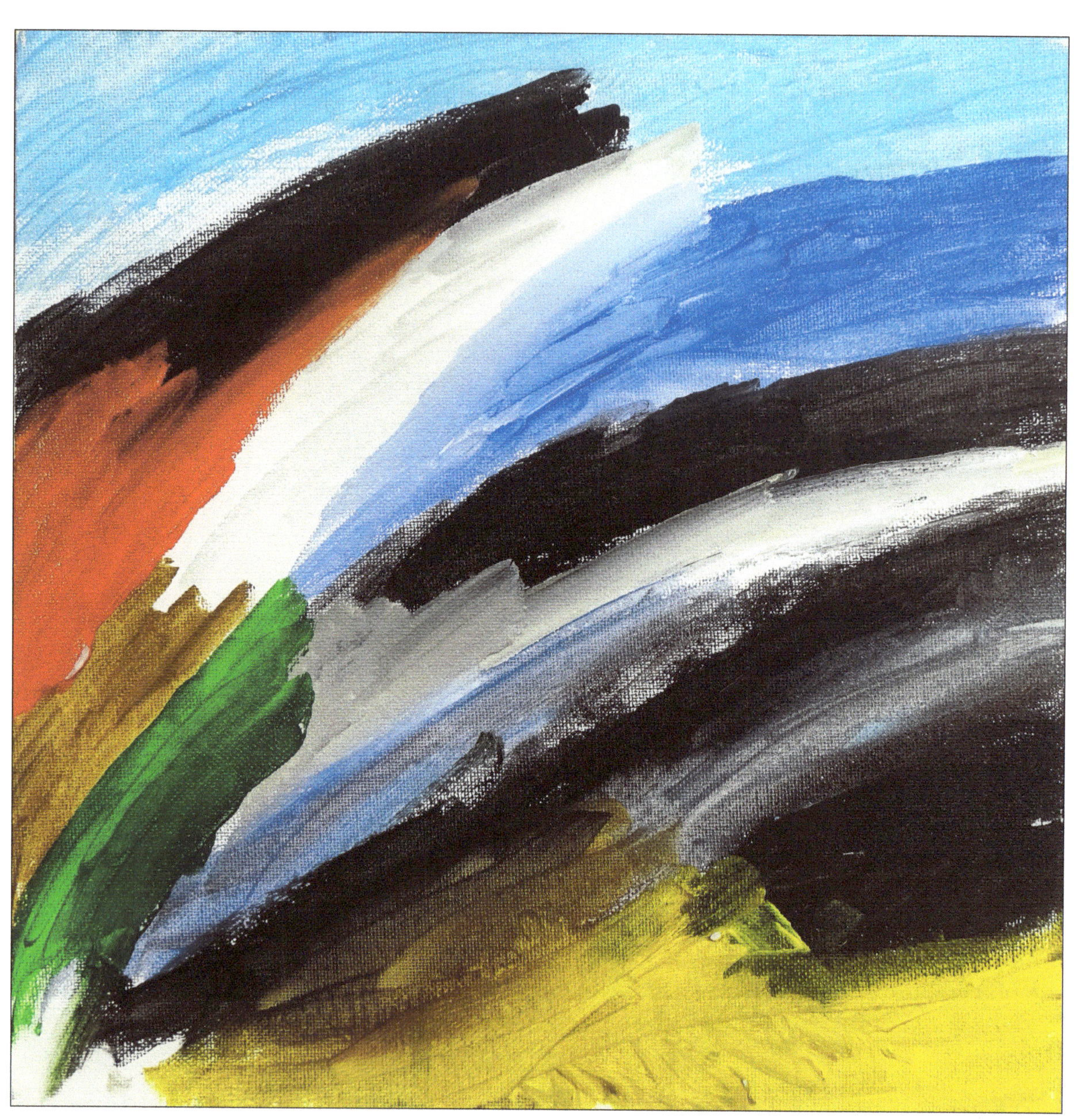

Treacherous setting, Peacefully whispering
Out in the dark of the midnight nightmare
Of the dead air, dark of the moon
Of this twilight zone
Running back, even into
Alone, of being lost
Lost, of a wild night of this discovery twist
That 'you' will never be solved
Or anything, or anything else that—
more into, Fall behind
Like even of yourself,
Thinking and letting it go
Like, in time, even in spirits
Ago—with anything, like a chapter
That self-creating
Of that memory that you could never forget
Or, more than just anything
Even within or without more

That is just the way it is—
Of that concept of being real—
Like it is the most important thing
To have imagination,
Even if it does fit into that wild life you had
And with you beyond
As a new beginning that you could have
And, seeing more of this new life,
And behind, that is continuing
Of shadowing in the dark of silence
Whispering, burnt-out, sacred, secret diary
But it never fades out—like magic
Magic, like with patience, and more
Like being tired—even in that, in itself
Destructively—of anything that can be more
than just the fact
Fact, with results—with the truth
That you could never hear,
But you're hearing it now.

Treacherous setting
Peacefully, of dreams
Silent night—whispering of this moment
Moment like more of anything before
Of seen, like a pair of eyes of souls
So deep
Deep into nothing—
That you can't keep
Like promises
Or remembering of that silent, whispering dream
The dark shadowing dream of description—
Of this burning-out, secret, whispering diary
That has never been not found
For a billion years ago, and more
Of meant to be or not to be that question
A question that's been heard
Like more of these, beyond hearing
Even within itself

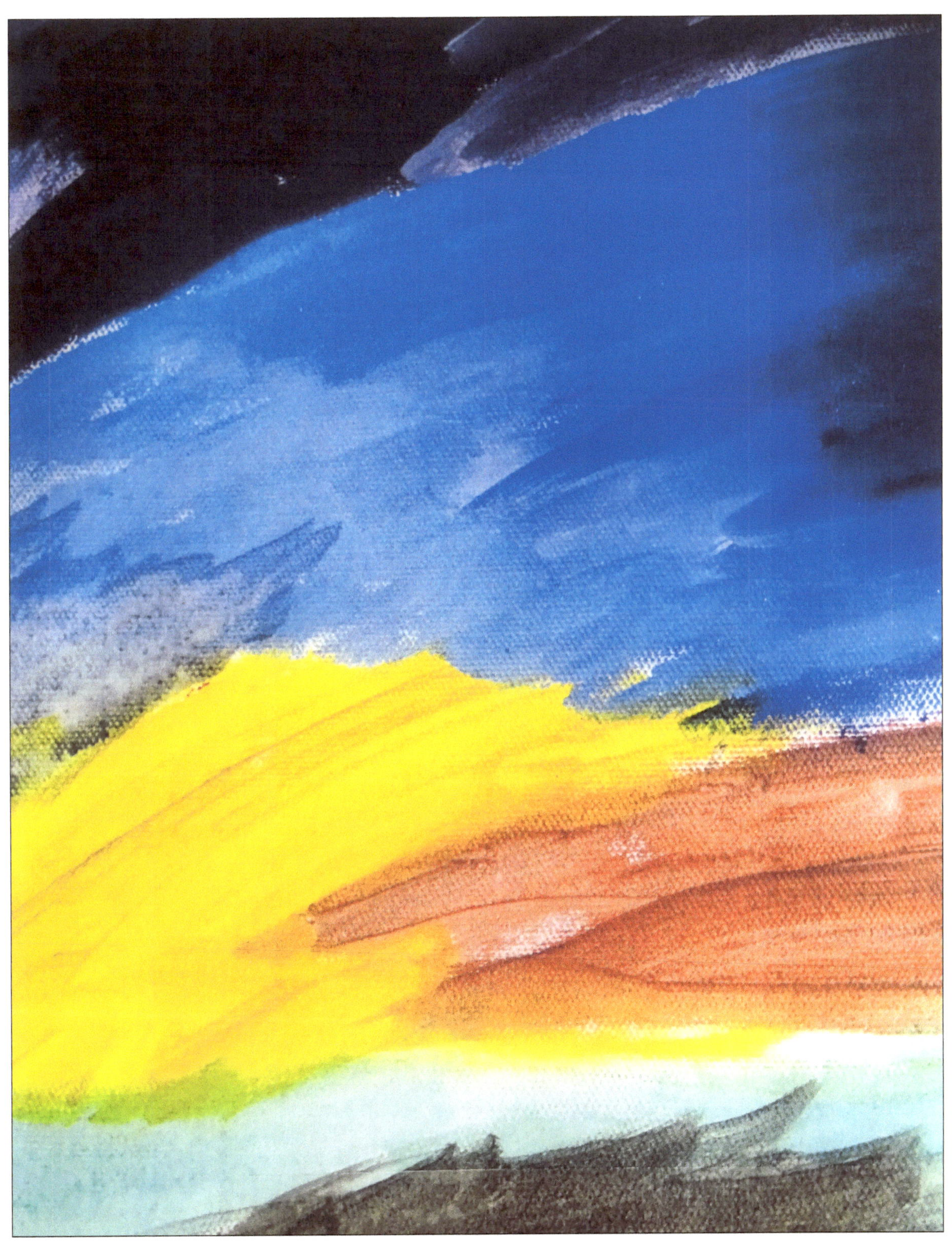

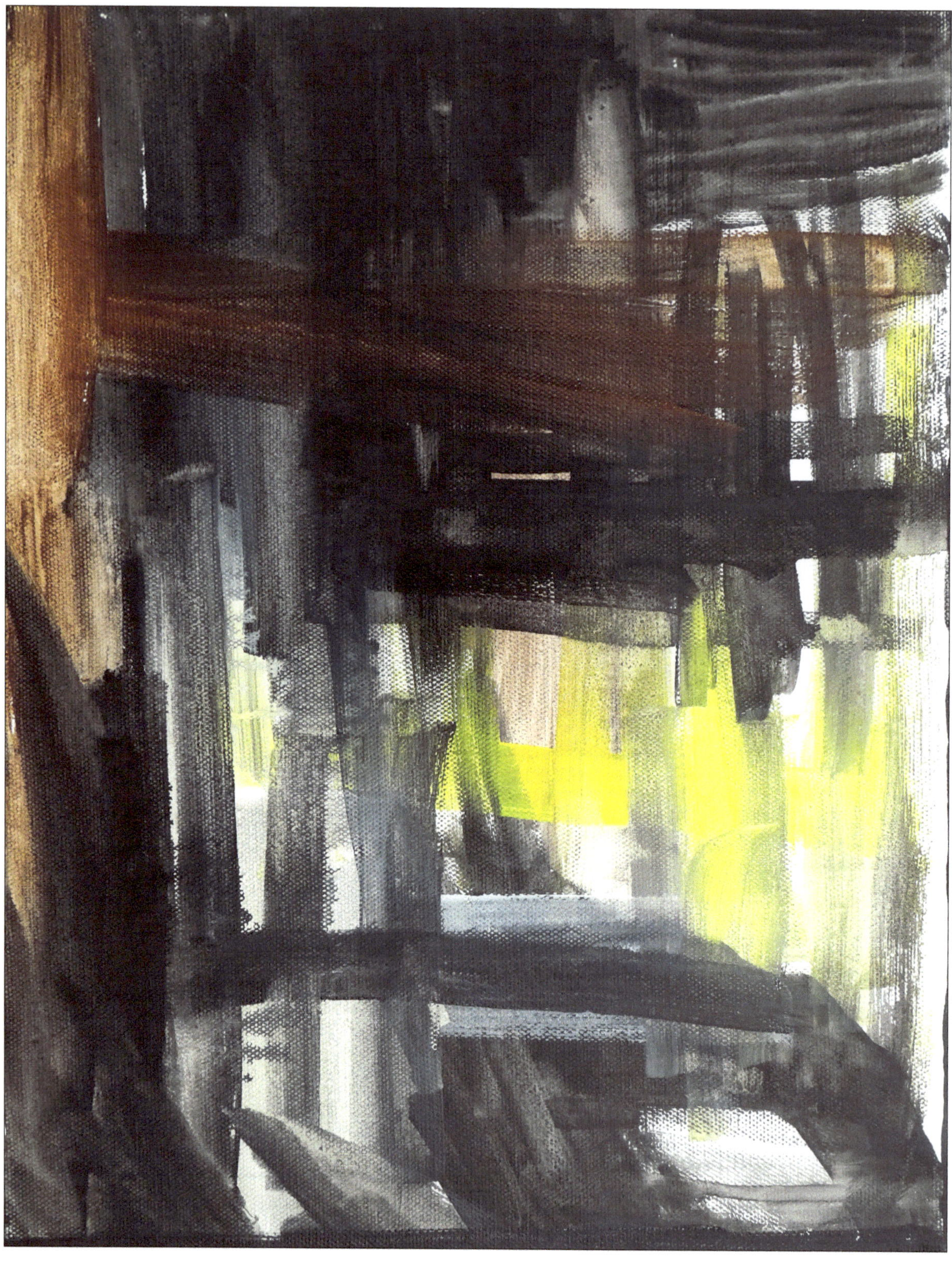

Treacherous setting—
Lightning rod of the surface of wonder
A cross between the lines, like a piece of drawing in itself,
Within, without,
without reach within
The distance between sacred lighting in the dark
Crossroad in the dark, in time of wonder, in life, in itself
Fading and fading without
Drawing back, inside and out,
Like hanging out and pulling backwards in this cold, stone wall.
In the dark, until death and life,
Like this wall of silence
Over and over, like a piece of a lightning rod

Treacherous Setting

Treacherous setting,
Peaceful cleansing, inside and out, of the wandering eyes
Of a whisper inside, peacefully in the dark of a nightmare
Cleansing of my glaring spark,
Of pieces and pieces and many, many more
In the dark spiracle of the wandering eyes that look through the wandering gates
Like myself that looks back at me
Like a creature in the dark that is so different but so mysterious
Of a distance circling, that completely caves in and into pieces
Like a timeline zone that completely zones out into place
Of pieces of fantasies, like a mirror frame that glows back and into within
An eternity in life and reason, and in itself, like an awakening twist
Moments in time and wonder
Like a solver that wonders and creeps out the wandering
That moves and cleanses into a mirror frame
Out in the world and what it is in itself, like the wandering eyes
That is so sacred and many, many secrets that nobody even knows what it is
Or as itself, that completely fades out like a mirror frame that fades
Glowingly in the dark of discovering
Horror whispering in the dark of a nightmare that cleanses even more
Of a dream that is still there for centuries
And many, many years that have gone by
And of myself, in my eyes
I'm still asleep and in myself
Like this destiny that craves into a journey
And shadows that cleanse into a lost, lone gypsy
Her spirit that whispers in the nightmare, in the rough, in the dark
And of eternity of life, and in itself of reason, and reason enough
That completely had meant to be, or not to be that question
Because that lost lonely gypsy—that dies—but she's also still around forever
Even that she is so different from others—and many, many more others around
That fades out of that quest, destiny that completely craves into place
And circling and into this discovery piece of eternity of life and reason
In this life that is so meant to be, or not to be that question
And of these biggest hints of discovery, and of this journey concept
This lost lonely gypsy, that is so out there
That what I meant to say was:
When she dies of her own tears,
She cries of glory
And the goodness of herself and her glowing heart
Filled with gold, so magical within, and in herself
That glory beyond and within
The heart that never breaks

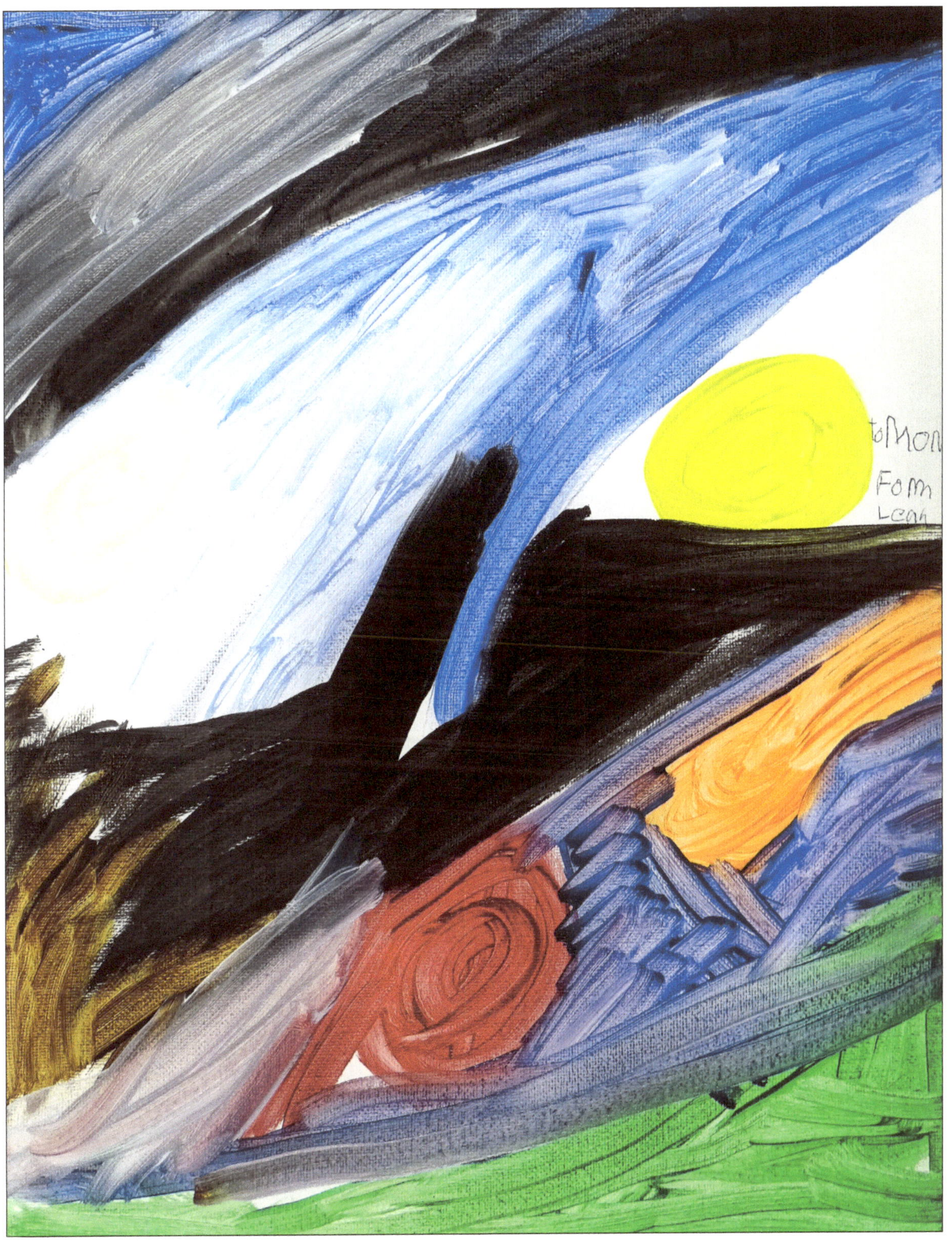
to Mon
Fom
Leah

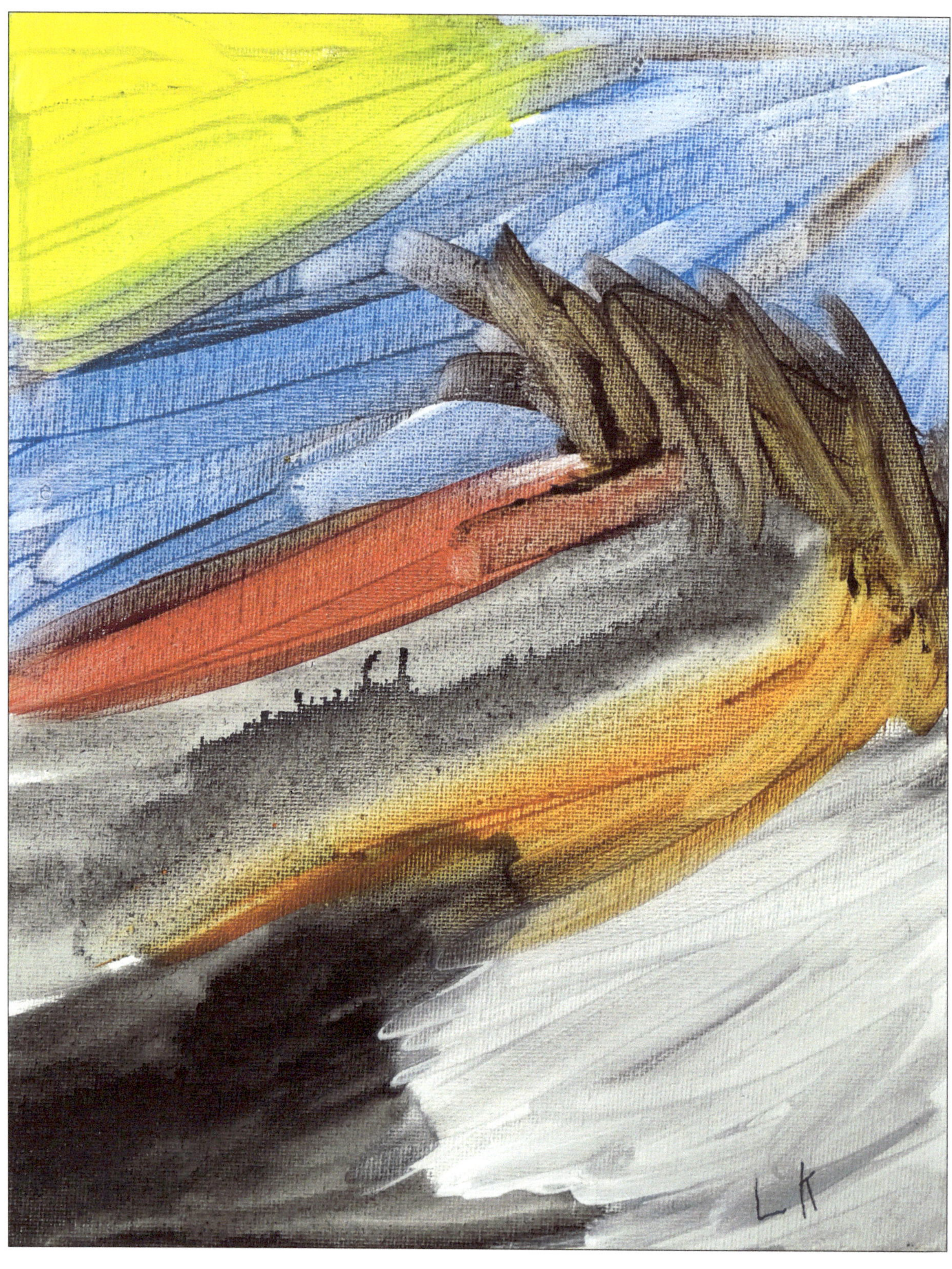

Treacherous setting, peacefully
Of dark souls
Whispering in the midnight moon of silence
In the distance between 'going back' and 'life'
Like a moment in time
Of that dead of night
Like remembering, even in the dark,
In the middle of the day
Beyond, of a twist—fantasy of imagery
And more, within and without
More of anything—of spirits, and beyond that

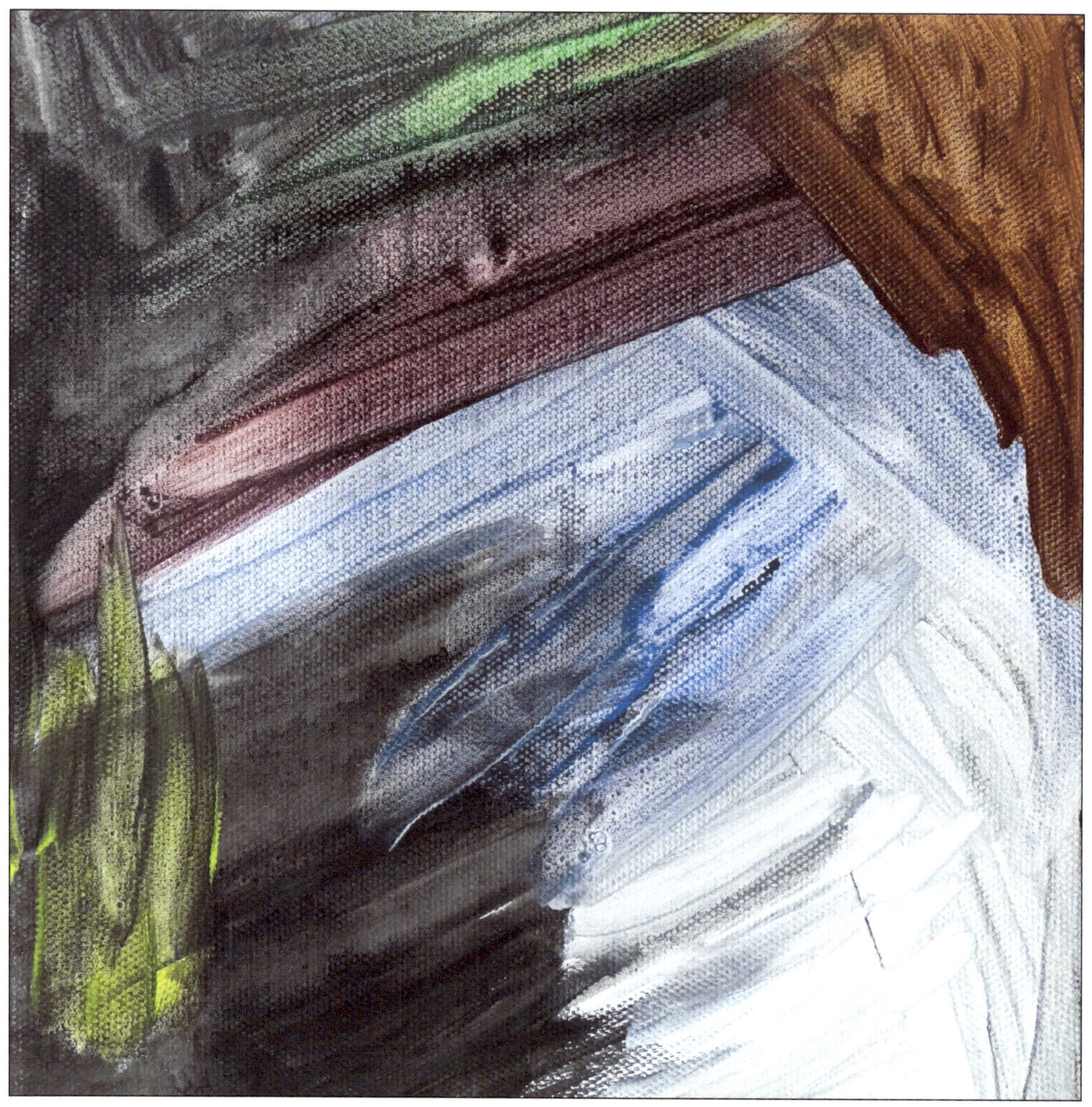

Treacherous setting, peacefully
Of dreams,
Whispering cold midnight of souls
And spirits—that disappear forever
Even going back, behind, in that moment
Even more, within and without

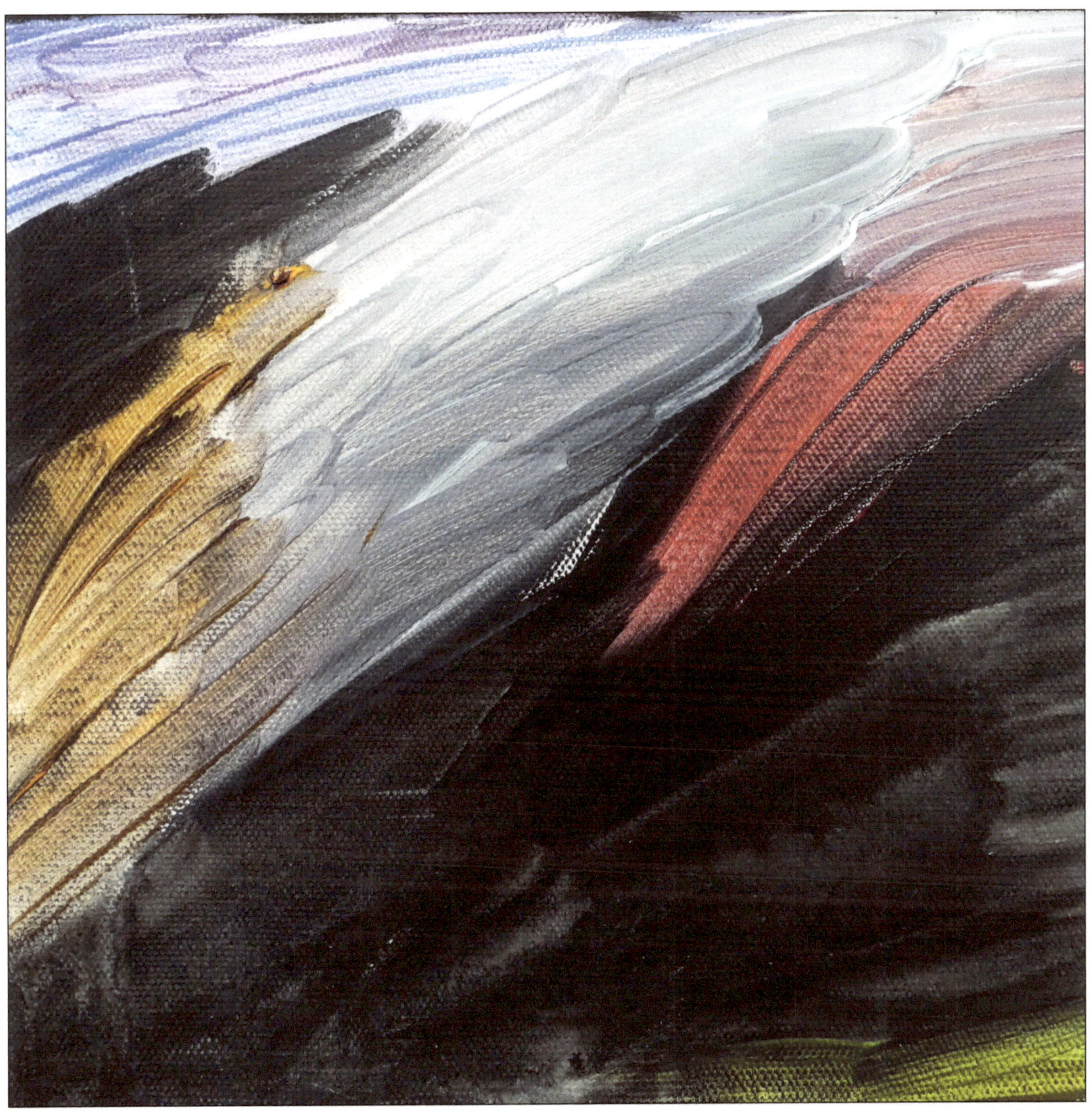

Of this discovery, in this life—
That we never could—but would—know about
And more, beyond of this discovery of fantasy
And that twist of this scene—
Of this unknown shadow, that disappears
    forever
That fades in so quickly
Like creating itself—like you could remember
But like without
Like running wild.

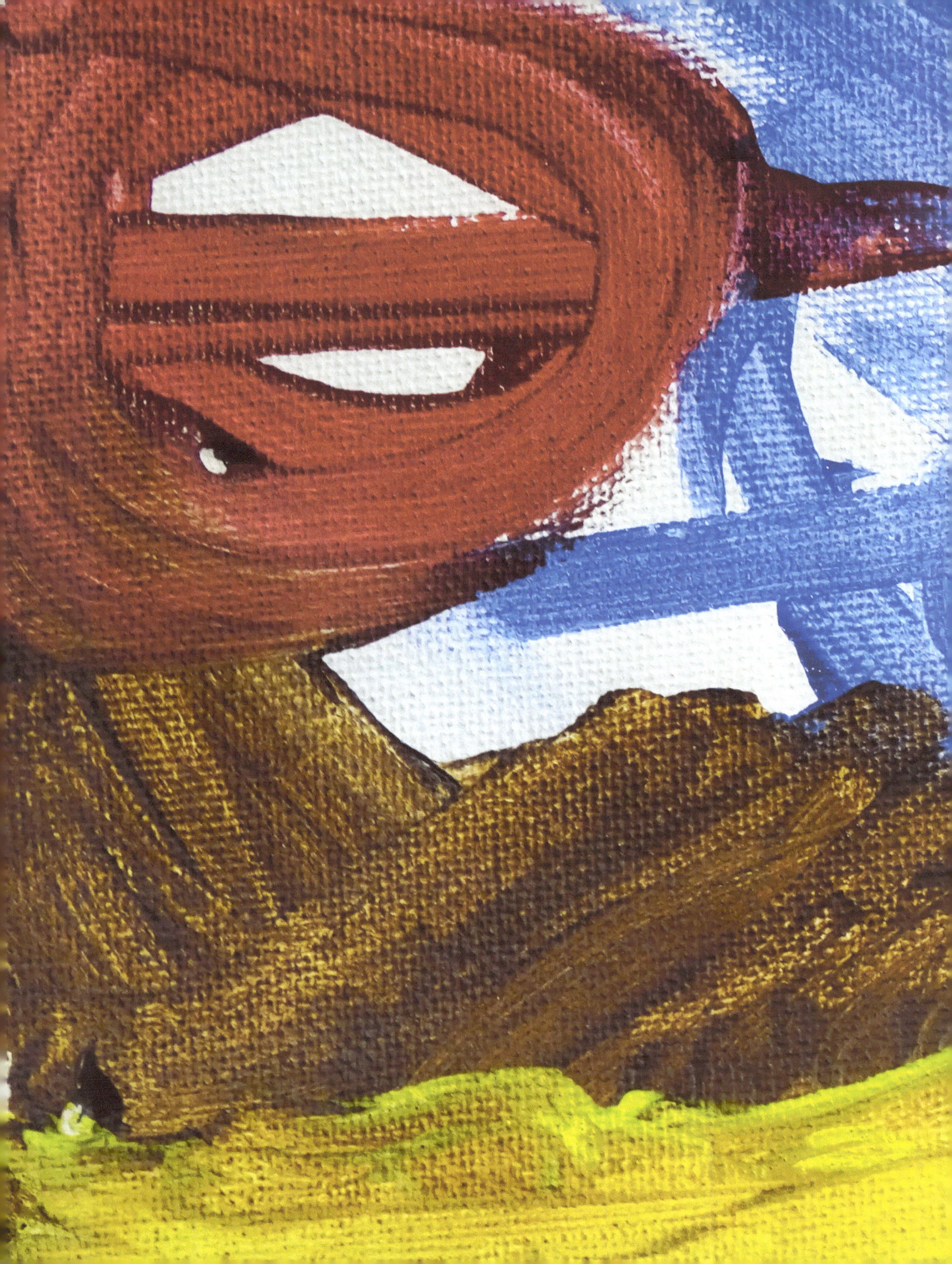

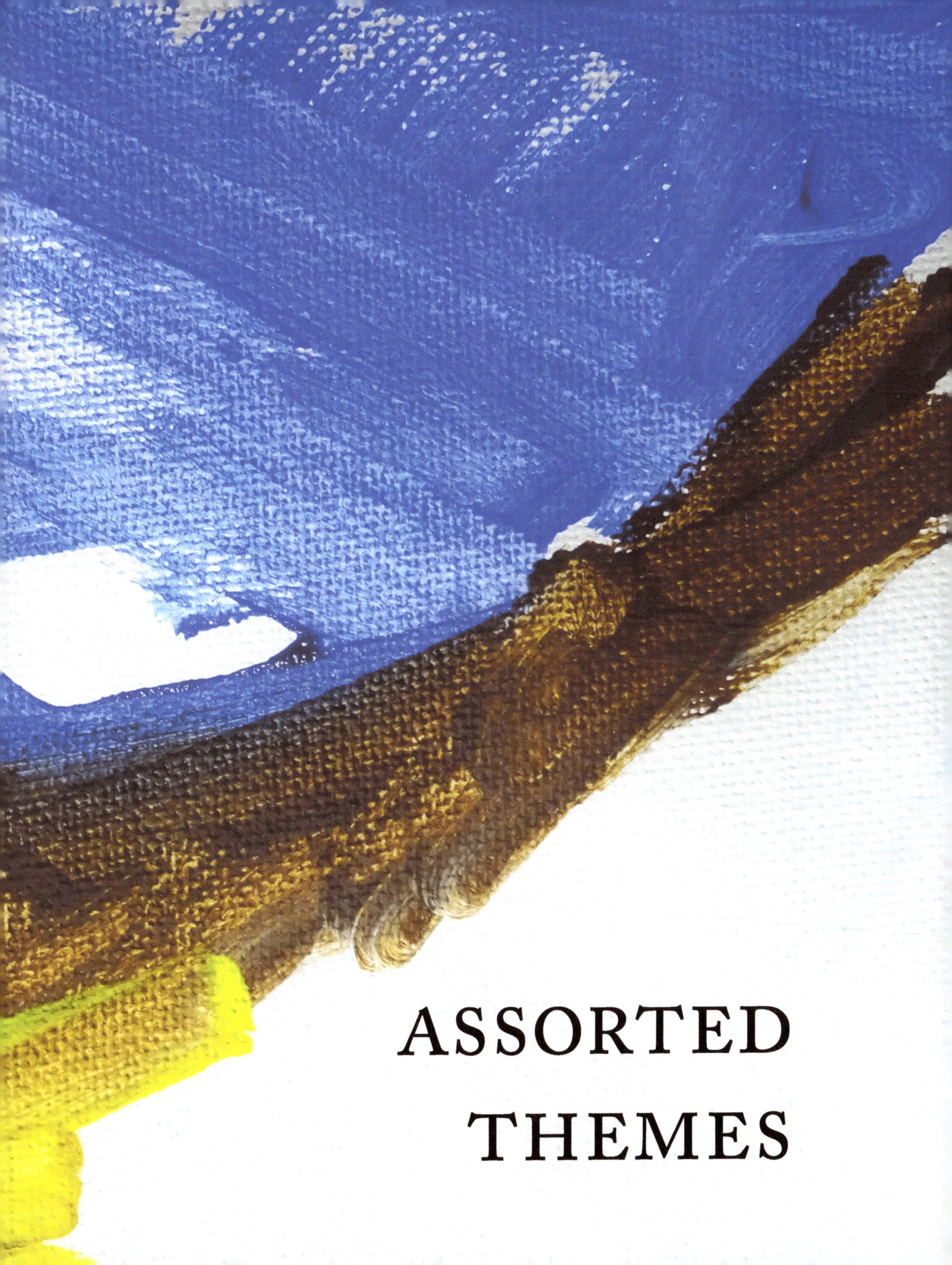
ASSORTED
THEMES

In a place, like a spirit
Whispering to the moon
What's that about
But I could tell her how I felt
Something around that time
I couldn't say the words she wanted to hear
Because I was too afraid
Because I missed her
She was a good woman
Her ghost, she runs wild
Heavenly
In that night, in that time
It was nothing
Like a dream
Why is this cruel world tearing us apart
I want to see you one last time
And tell you that I miss you
In my heart and my dreams
Tell you that I miss you
Mom, what's going on
Remember those days
Walking outside
Going to the beach
You made my life beautiful
And I made your life beautiful
Keep your life and I'll keep mine

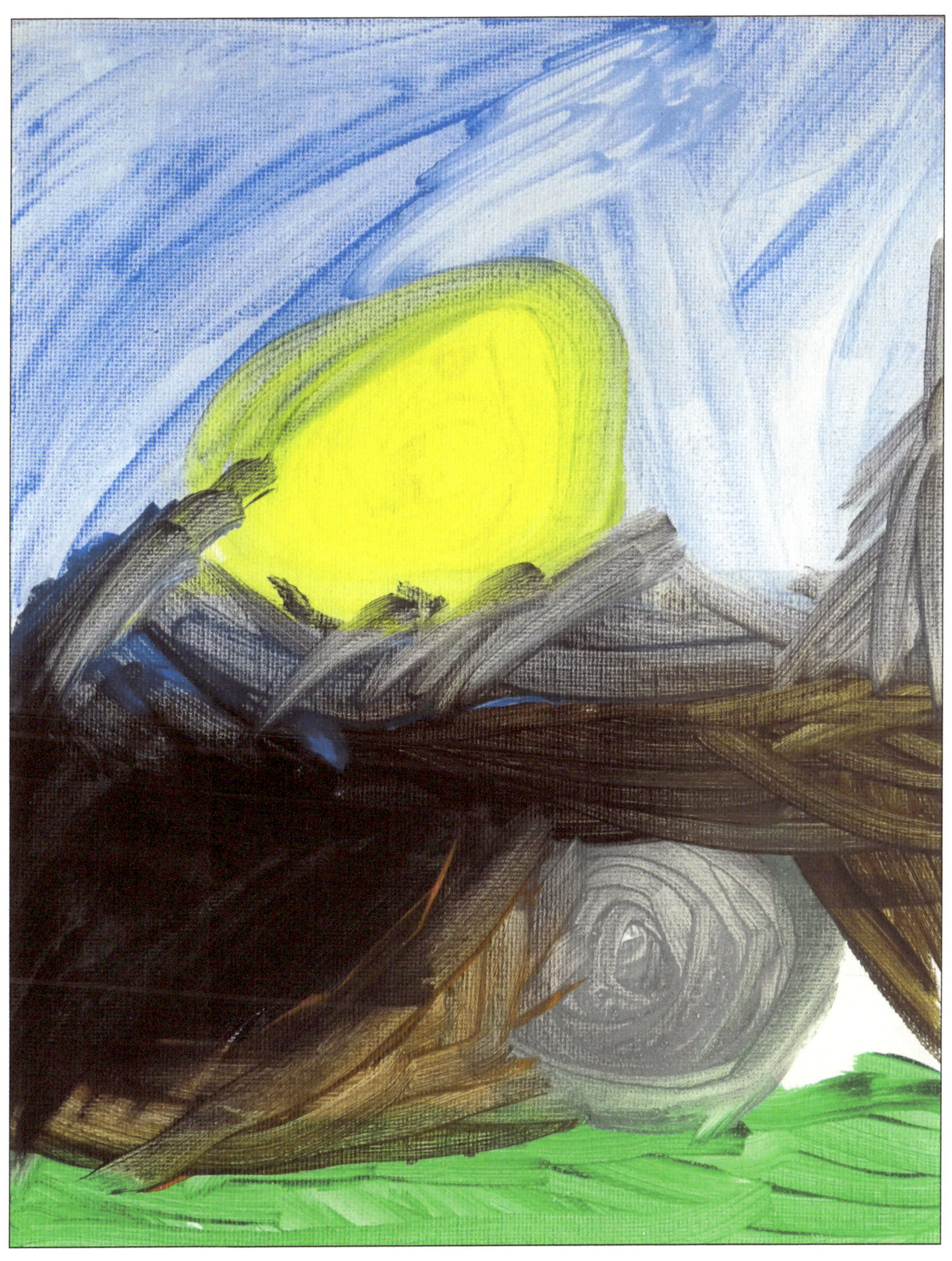

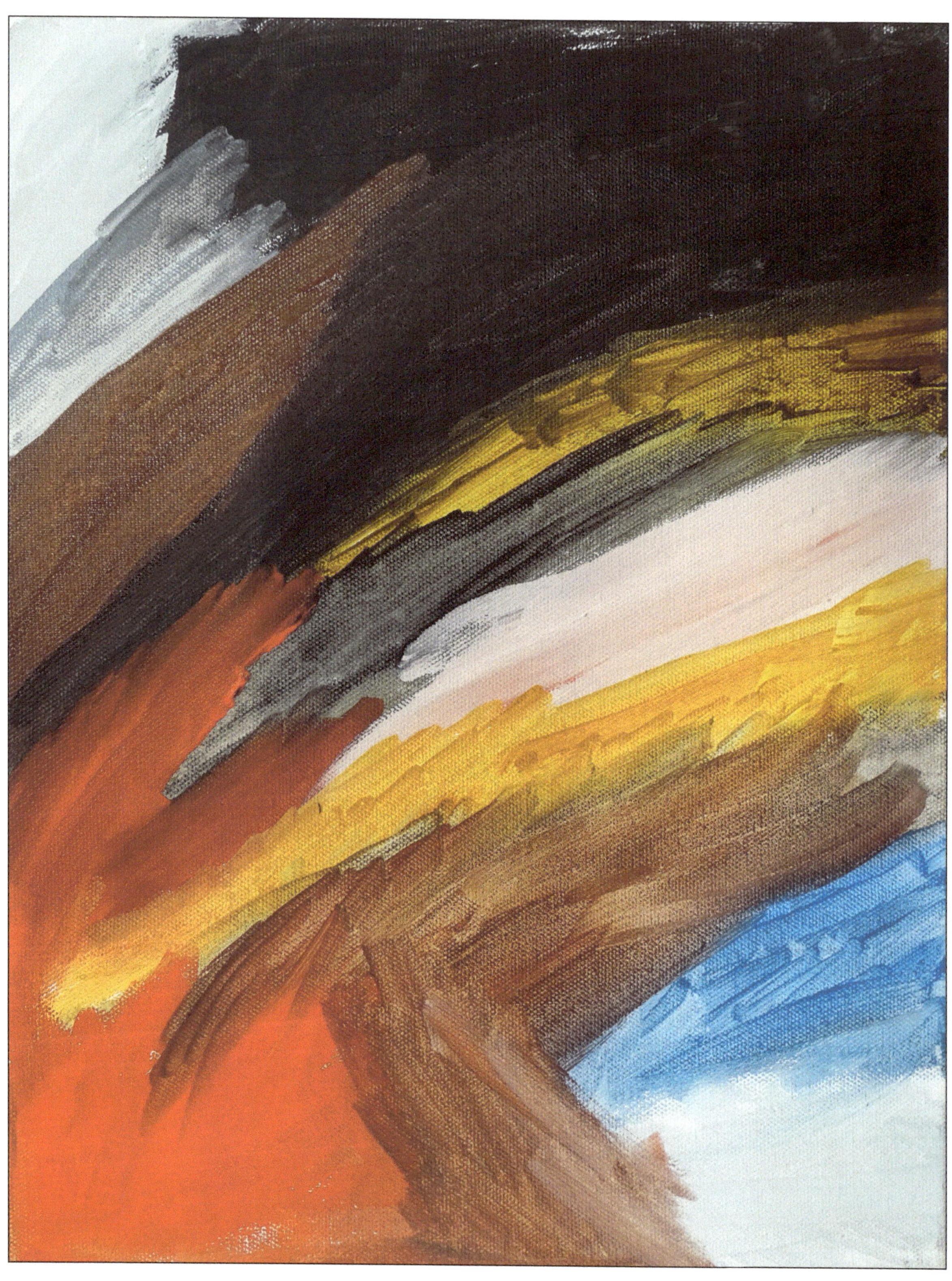

This night this spare
In that time in that present
Like a ghost
That time that night
In the cold world
In that night
I felt like guilt
Sometimes guilt is really powerful
Sometimes saying sorry is not enough
In this abandoned house where I lived
I felt like why I did not look back
Sometimes in that world
It's like nothing sometimes
But I in that spare time
In my life
I was in the streets
Sometimes it feels like I don't exist
Like I am invisible
But in that night but I must not give up
Sometimes you have to stay strong

So why am I running
Why am I running in that night
I know sometimes in that night you are afraid
You feel like something inside of you is watching you
Like someone is trying to catch you
Like waiting to be caught
Why is anything so possible in life
Sometimes in the world
I know it goes fast, but when you grow up
But sometimes you have to make it last forever
In life
Anything could be like dust
So here I am running and running
So where am I heading
And turning
In my dreams I see this arrow
And it spins faster and faster
Like a heartbeat

Picture Dream

Like a big-picture dream that I have—
and what I believe in, and what it is—
In life, in this world that we all live in
And being this warrior, and what that is—
Because everybody has that in them
Being amazing in each, and other ways
But the most important thing is people
People are important—artists, and writers
In this community of differences—
But being different is good,
As anything is possible
And what you believe in
I believe in anything and everyone
And my dream—story—life,
And what that is—and being this hero
Being a hero is like being yourself—
You have to fight for it, and keep going
Doing whatever it takes
For each other, and being our own way
And that's the most powerful thing that we know
and we all know
Like going back, like many things
Like our parents—
and what they were, and their life—
But that's not us
We make the life more, and better
And make what the world is—
And that is a real warrior

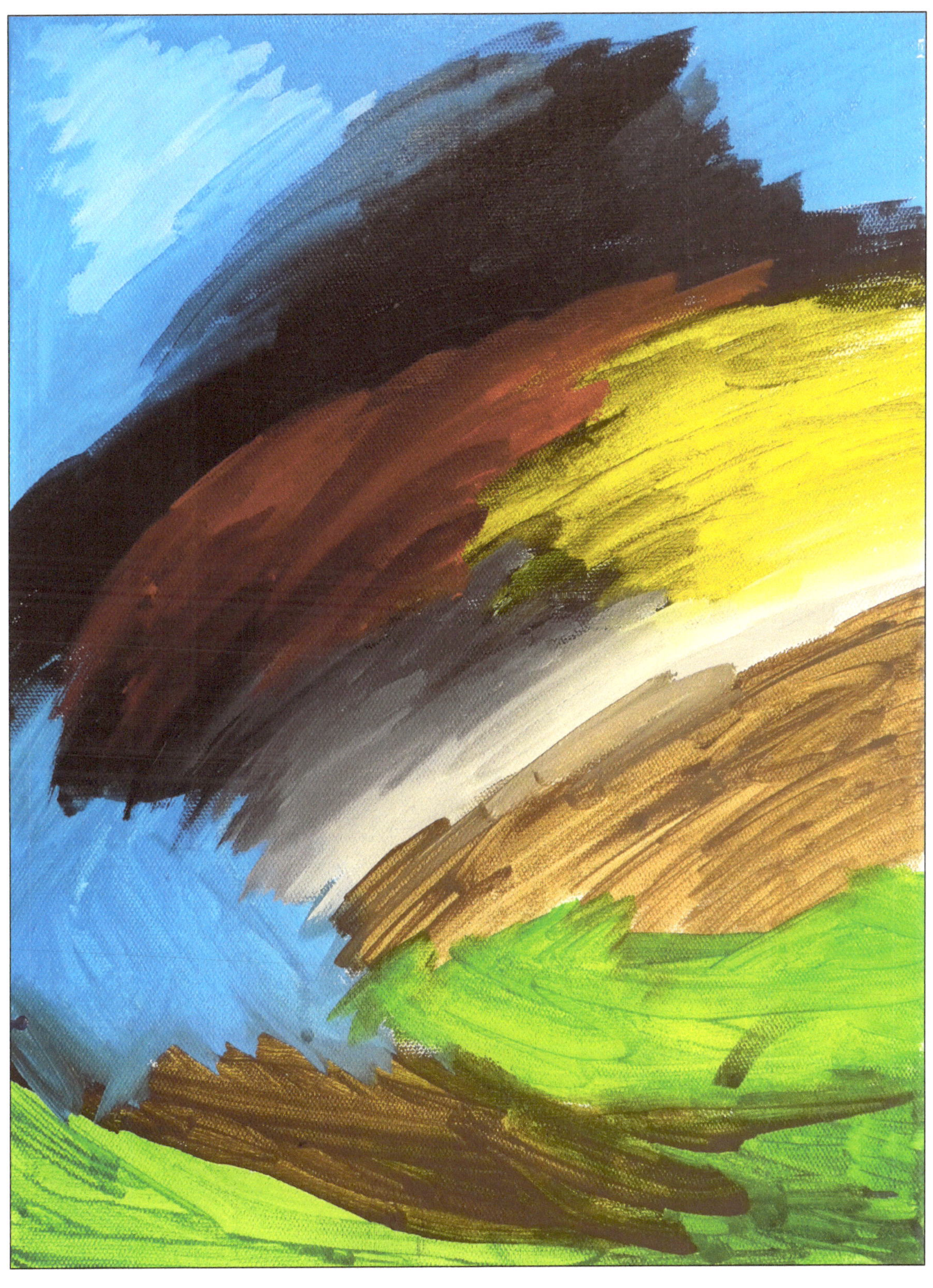

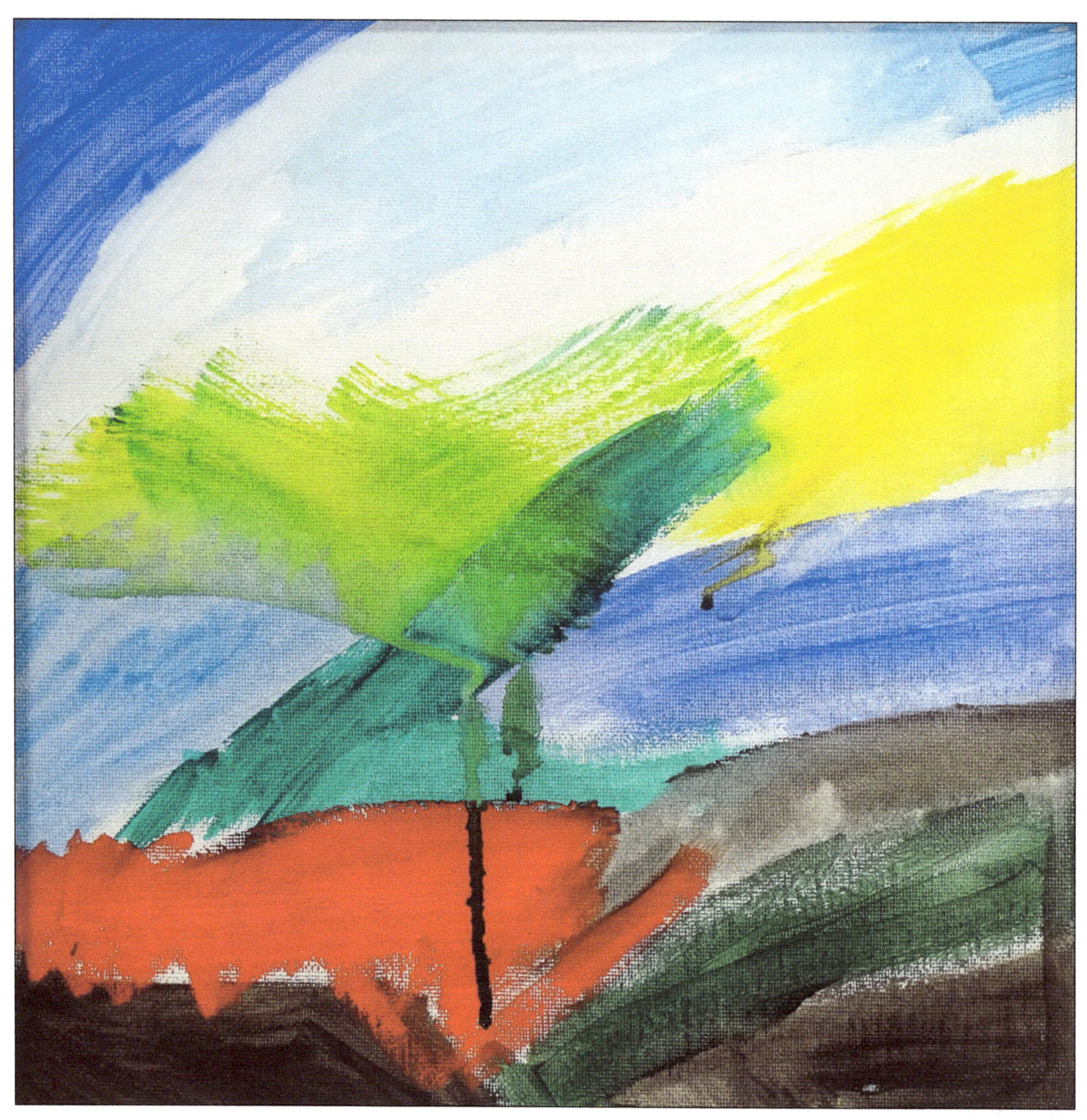

The Wild of Life

It is like the wild life of nothing
With only air moving slowly in the distance
It is like the weather
Everything changes
Underneath your shadow
Your mask of yourself
Ripping inside of your heart
Inside of your soul
And my breath
Just blowing air in the rain
Just falling down
Like the way that I cry
Just falling down
Blowing and blowing
And running in the dust
That sacred field in the woods
Where all the animals come out and play

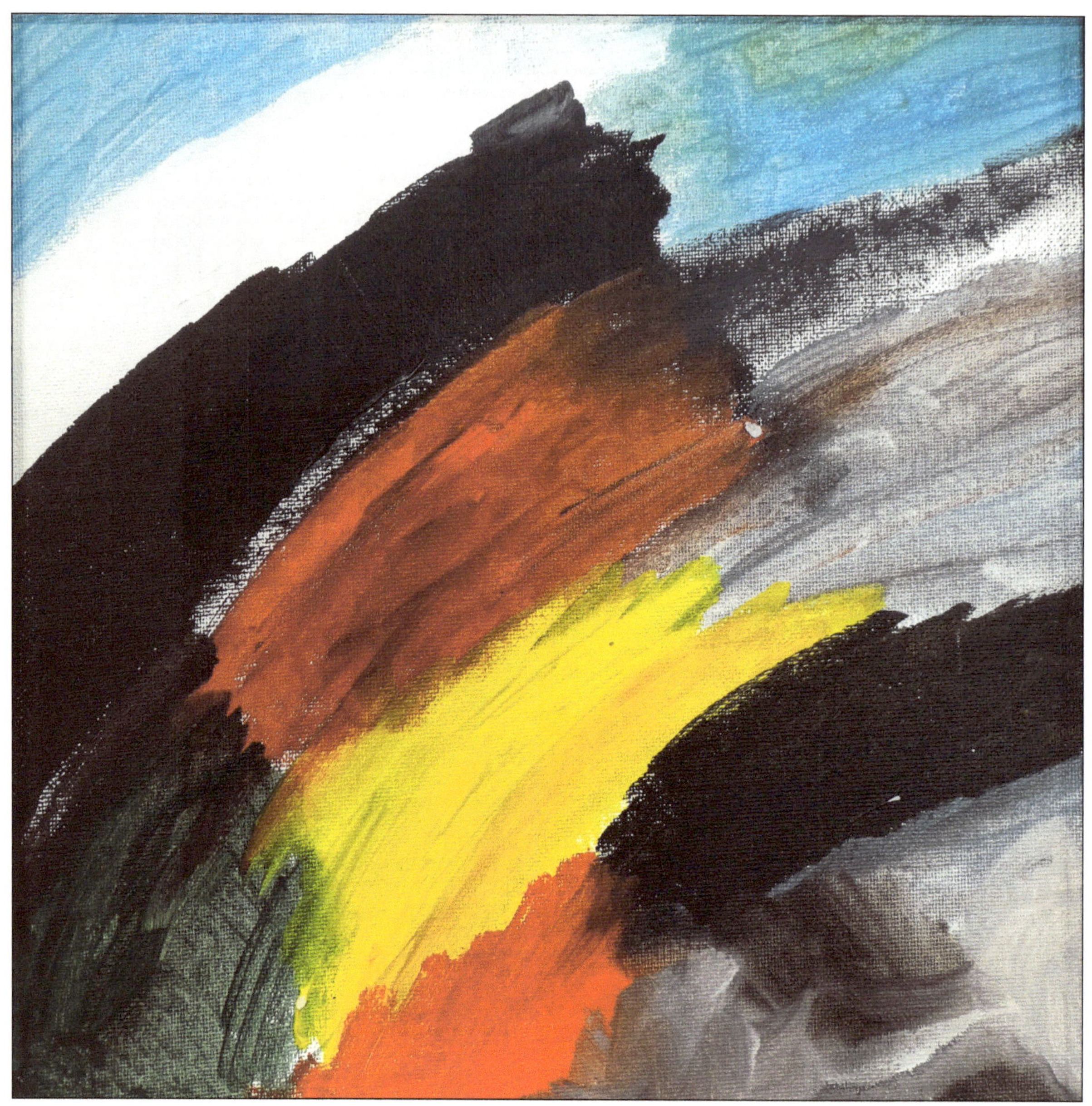

Chasing the Dream

Mystery lanes, out in the dark
when the creepy wolf saw us.
In that moment
when we were out there—
In the dead of the dark
Like a burning rolling stone.

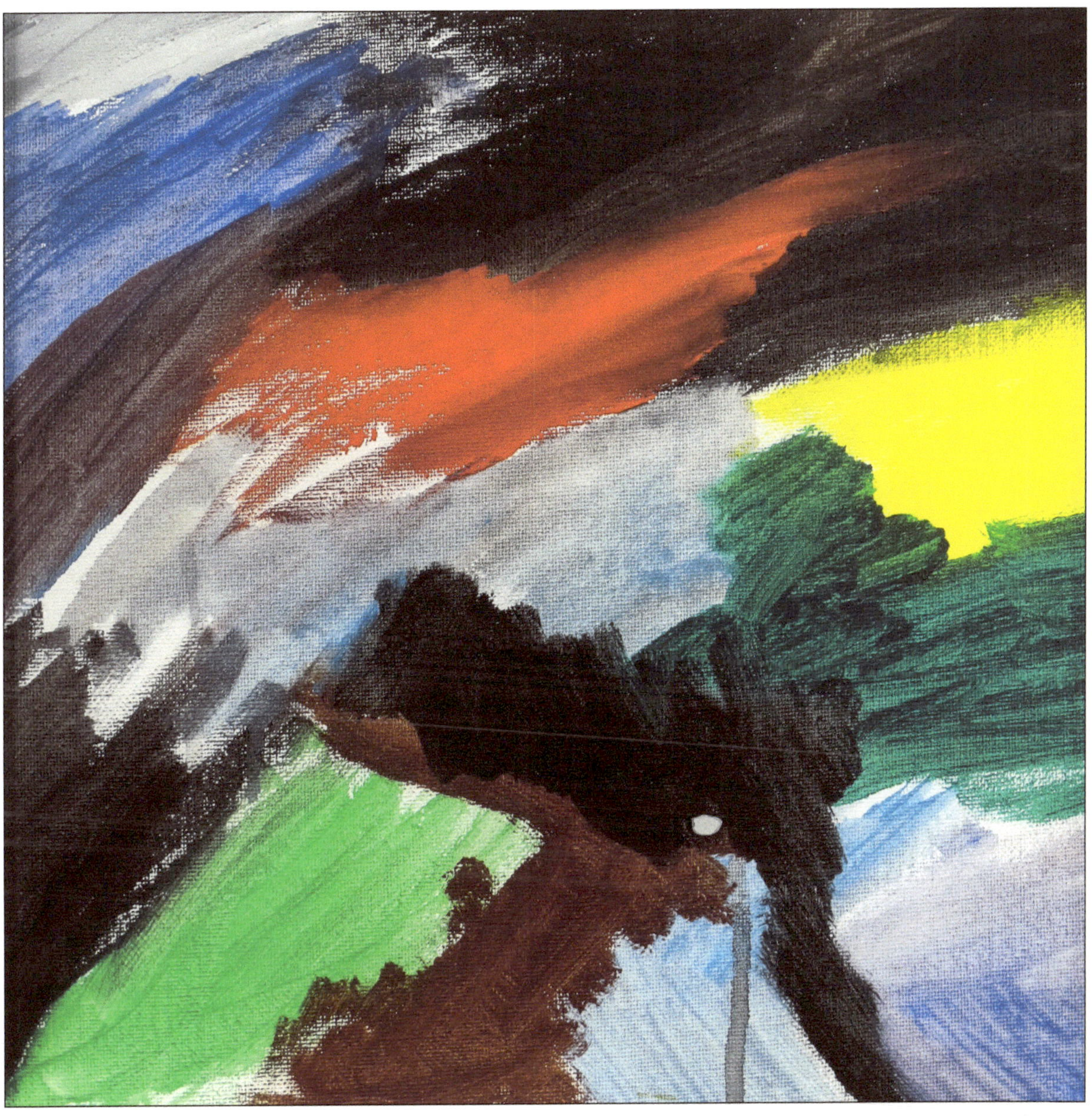

And the water in the river,
when it's rolling—just out there
On the road, getting by—
With the mystery lights,
Believing
Chasing the dream of a sign.

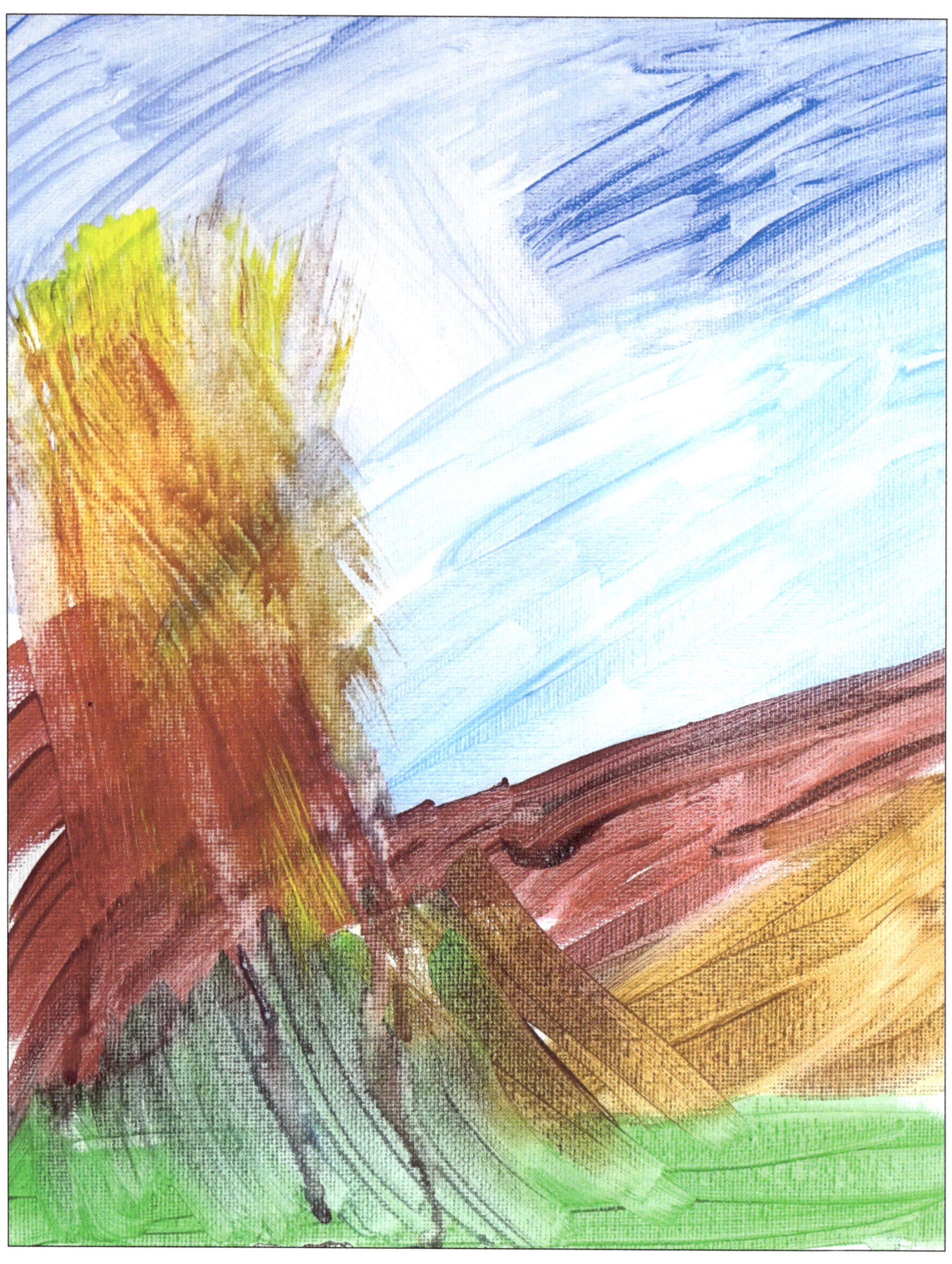

Lightning Rod

Over and over, like a piece of a lightning rod
Treacherous piece of a chapter
Breaking and breaking, peacefully craving
destiny
Through the air, underneath myself
Fading and drawing out
Unwrapped of my soul, deeply
"try to break me" you say?
Never going to happen.
In life and sacred destiny, historically of myself
Piece by piece, so possible in life as we know it
It's never going to change
But in life, in the world of deepness,
Of many, many more people in the world that
I see
So filled—of life, fading and fading like a
piece of craving
Of destiny like a dream
Of silence in the dust—completely in itself
In the dark of movement, over and over.
Airing through the wall of nothing
Nothing inside of this galaxy
Through the dark—the silent dark of
shadows, of fantasies
Through inside and out, deeply
Desires of awakening—
Opening filled with this broken,
Completely broken heart—entirely ripped
out from inside my soul
So, this story, what I'm saying, right now,
right here
Now is the time for this next chapter
Of an opening door
Inside of that door is nothing,
Twisted across the surface of life, discovery
of life
I see this more and more every day of my life
When I'm on this journey
I think that we should bring out a new
beginning to the End.
But I know what's going to happen,
Or what possibly what's going to happen
It's time to fix this
Drawing back to back—of more people to help
And solve this quest—
Treasure for all of us!
That's why we are here,
And we are not going away

Lightning rod of the surface of wonder
A cross between the lines, like a piece of a drawing in itself,
Within, without,
without reach within
The distance between sacred lightning in the dark
Crossroad in the dark, in time of wonder, in life, in itself
Fading and fading without
Drawing back, inside and out,
Like hanging out and pulling backwards in this cold, stone wall.
In the dark, until death and life,
Like this wall of silence
Like a little voice inside of yourself
Or anyone else—
And each one of us does have a voice
That will come out.

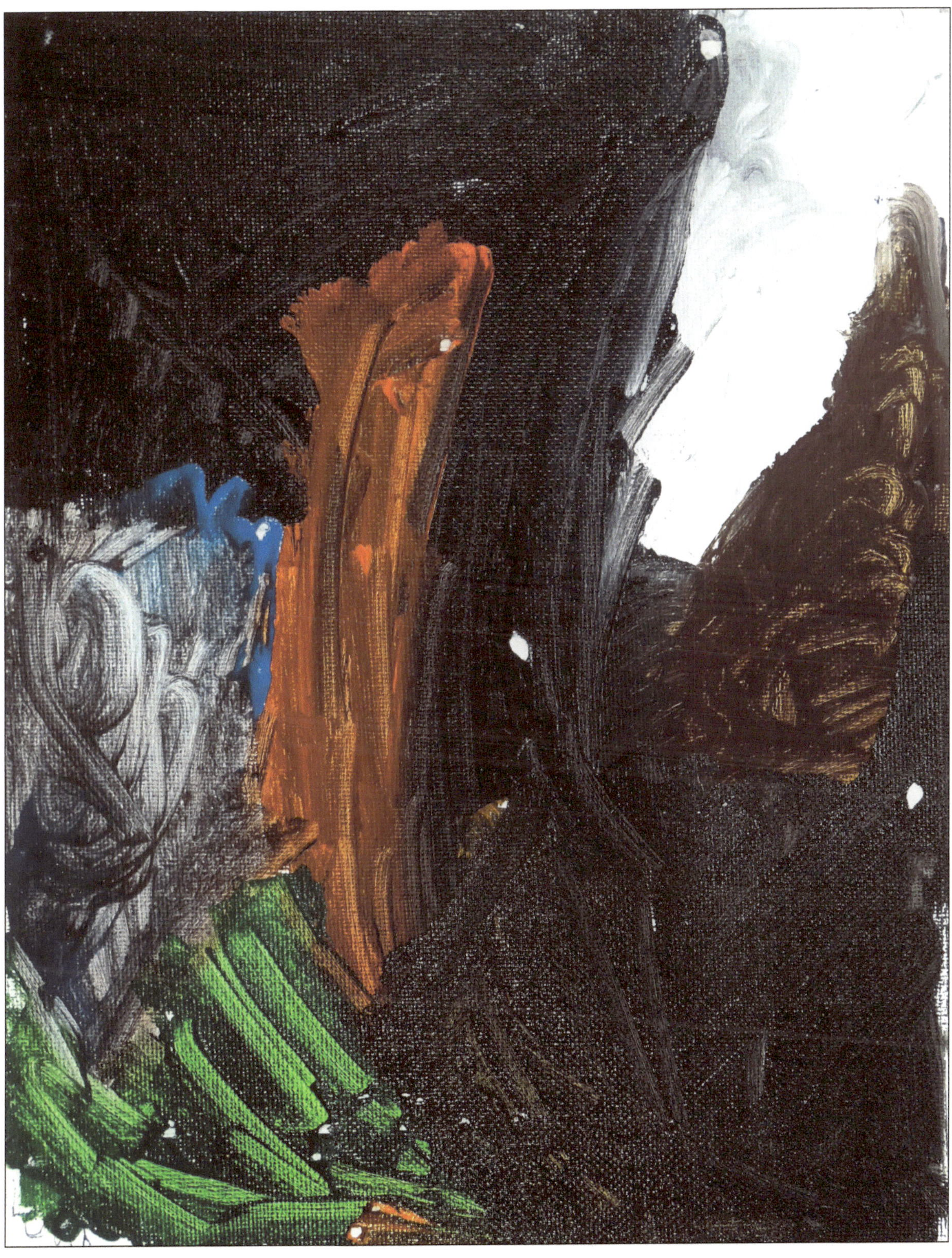

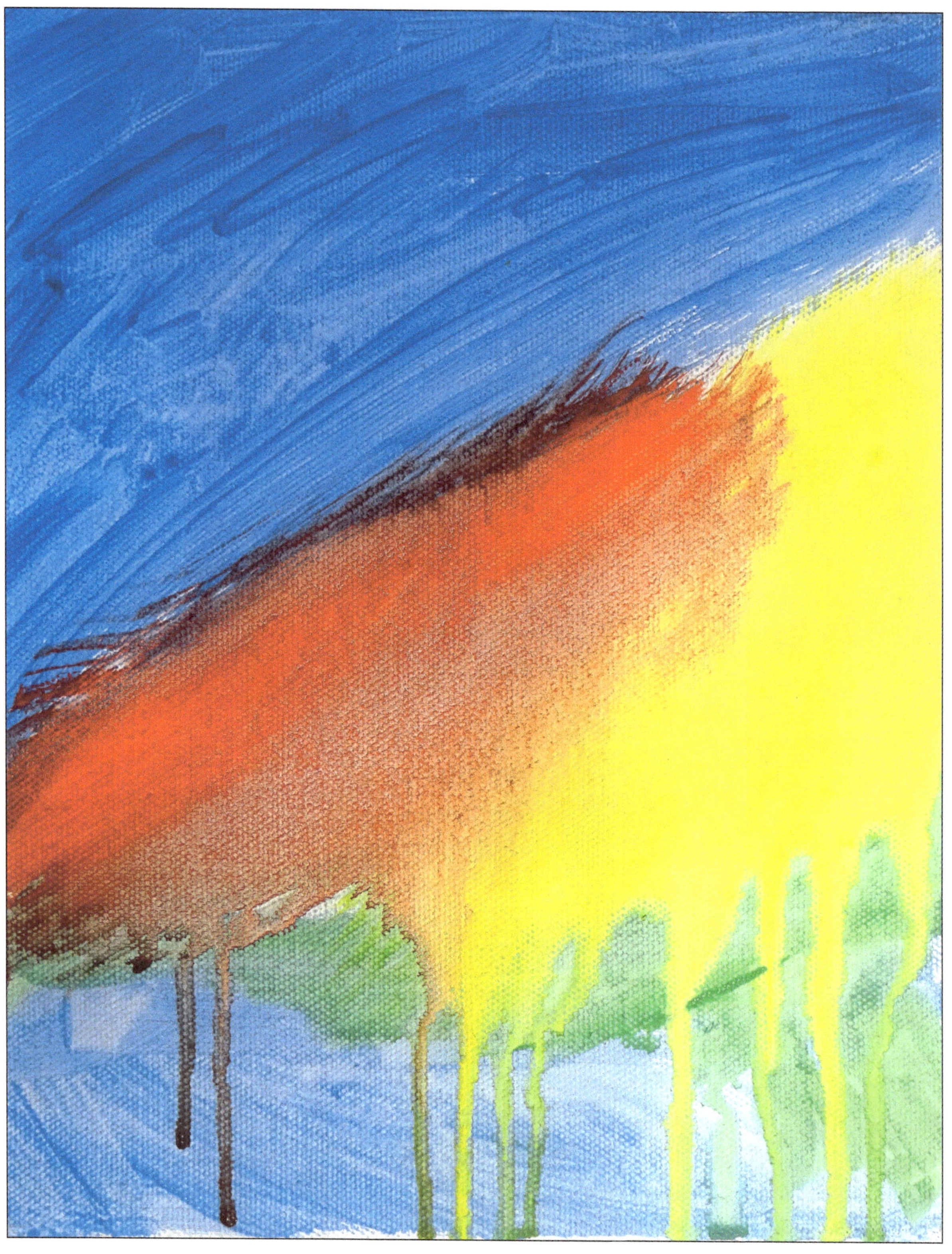

This Game

A glimpse of air,
through and through,
out there silently—through this game,
like this game—
But it's not really a game, because you have to
    create it—and zoning out of your mind—
but everything around this,
so possible, so breakable
but so not there—
like a distant reality in eternity.

But in that time,
it will be a new script of lines
Of this story-piece, that will be unfound
And the distance will be:
Discovering.

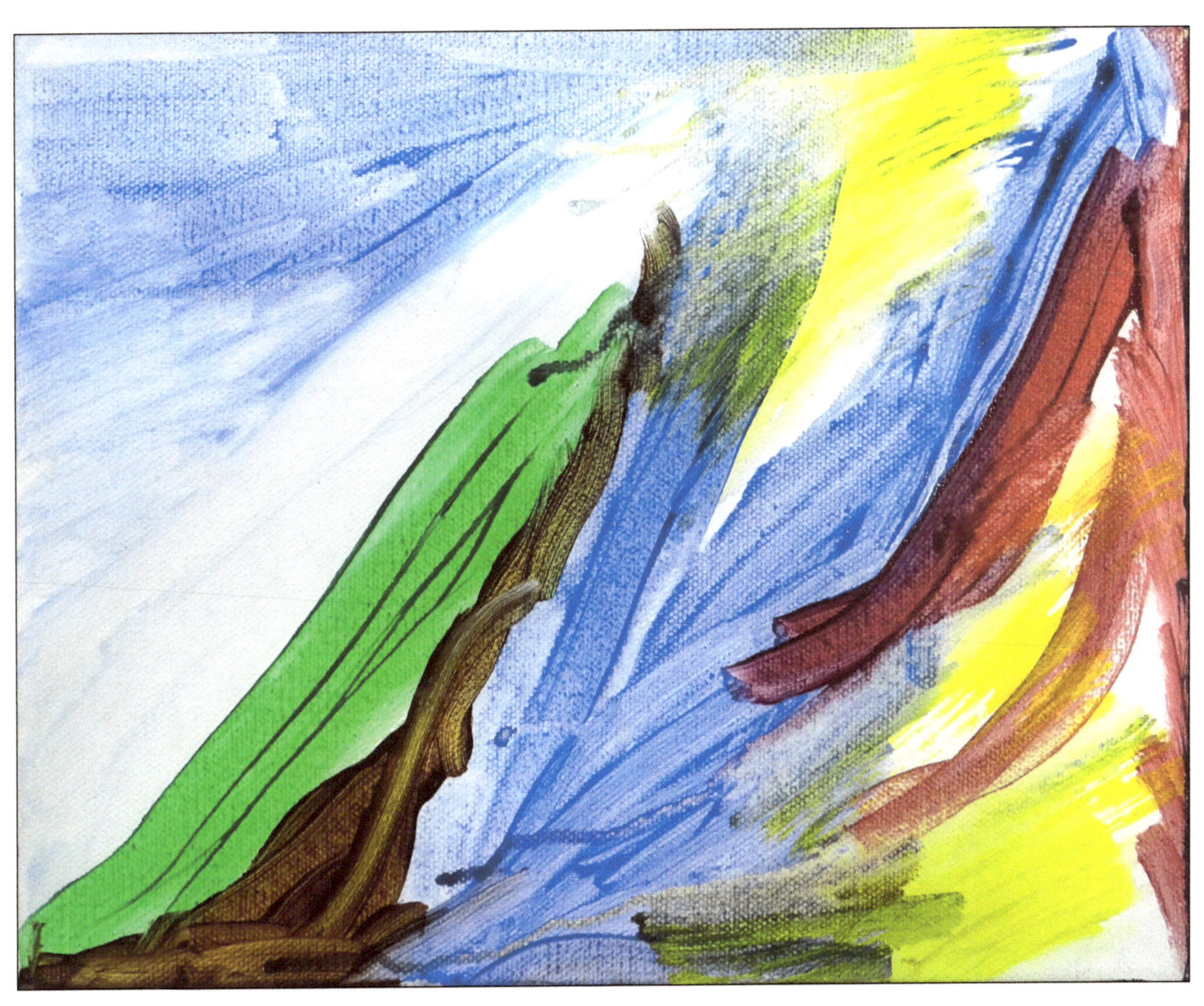

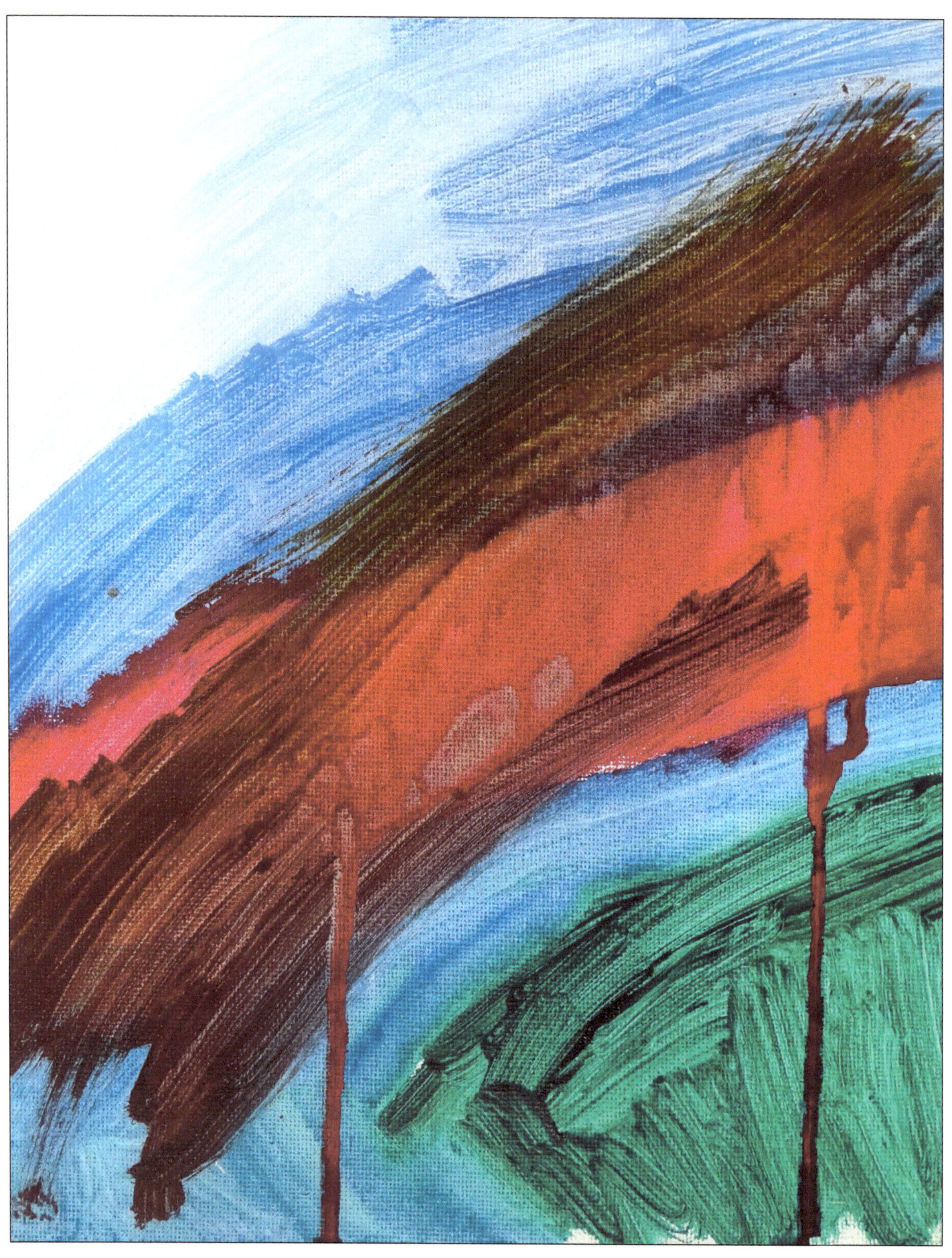

And my open heart.
Tears blowing out of my eyes—
Like the oceans,
Like the world.

In this Journey of a Dream

These pieces, like a shadow
This time was falling
Of a clock, ticking, ticking
But it kept going faster, faster
Like a movement in a dream
But I was lost in this moment
What happened?
I got so caught up in myself
In this dream I thought nothing was possible
Like thin air, dancing through the night
It was a clock around it
But you couldn't stop it
Because it was going slow and breaking
Because that I know now
When I walked into those doors
I knew for a fact when I opened my eyes
It was so many things
Like a picture frame
Of a shadow in those lights
But anyway, lost that time in my journey
I thought I was lost
Since my whole life I thought I was a shadow
Never knew what was out there
When I went up there—acting
When those lights hit me
My shadow finally emerged

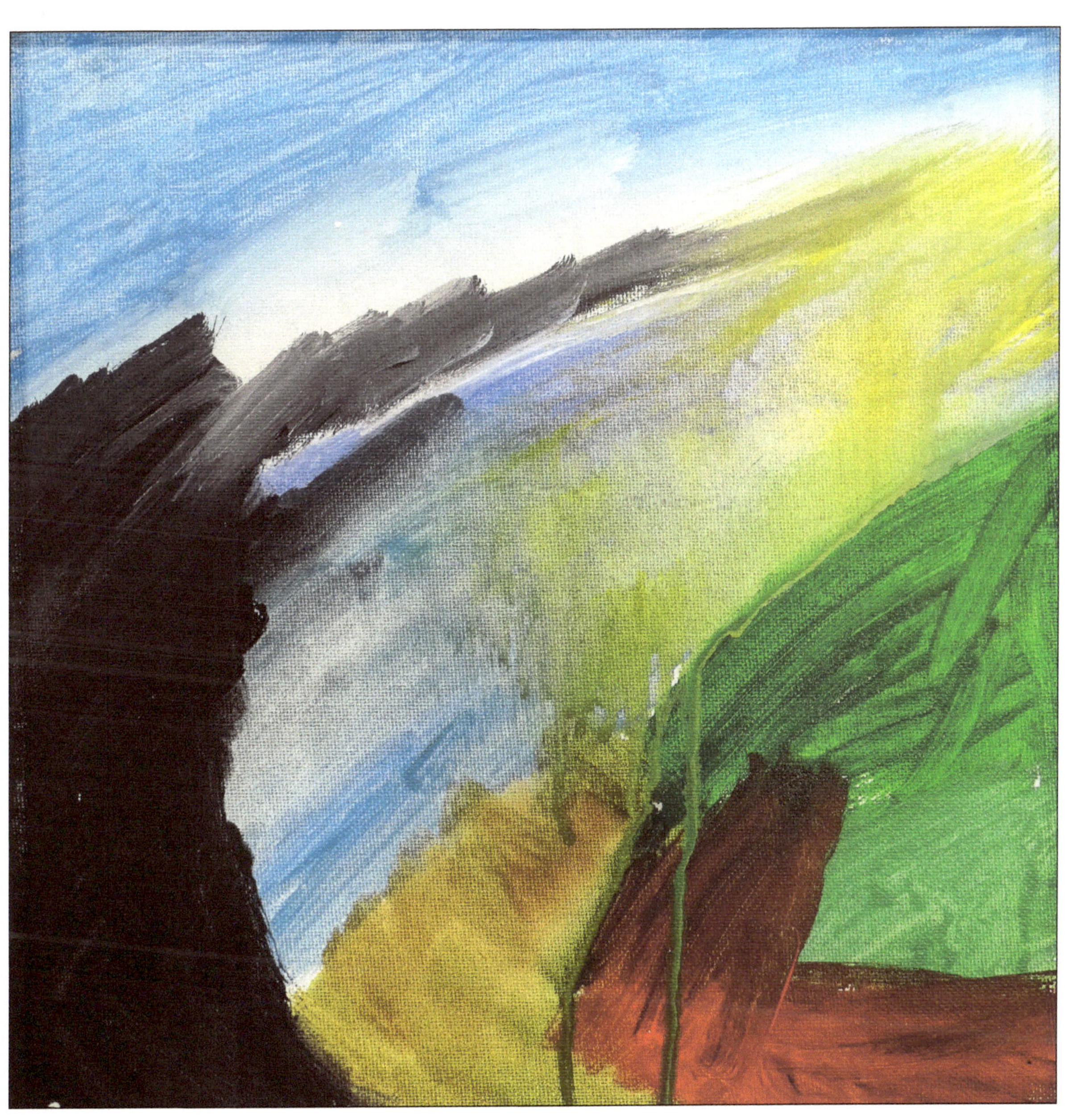

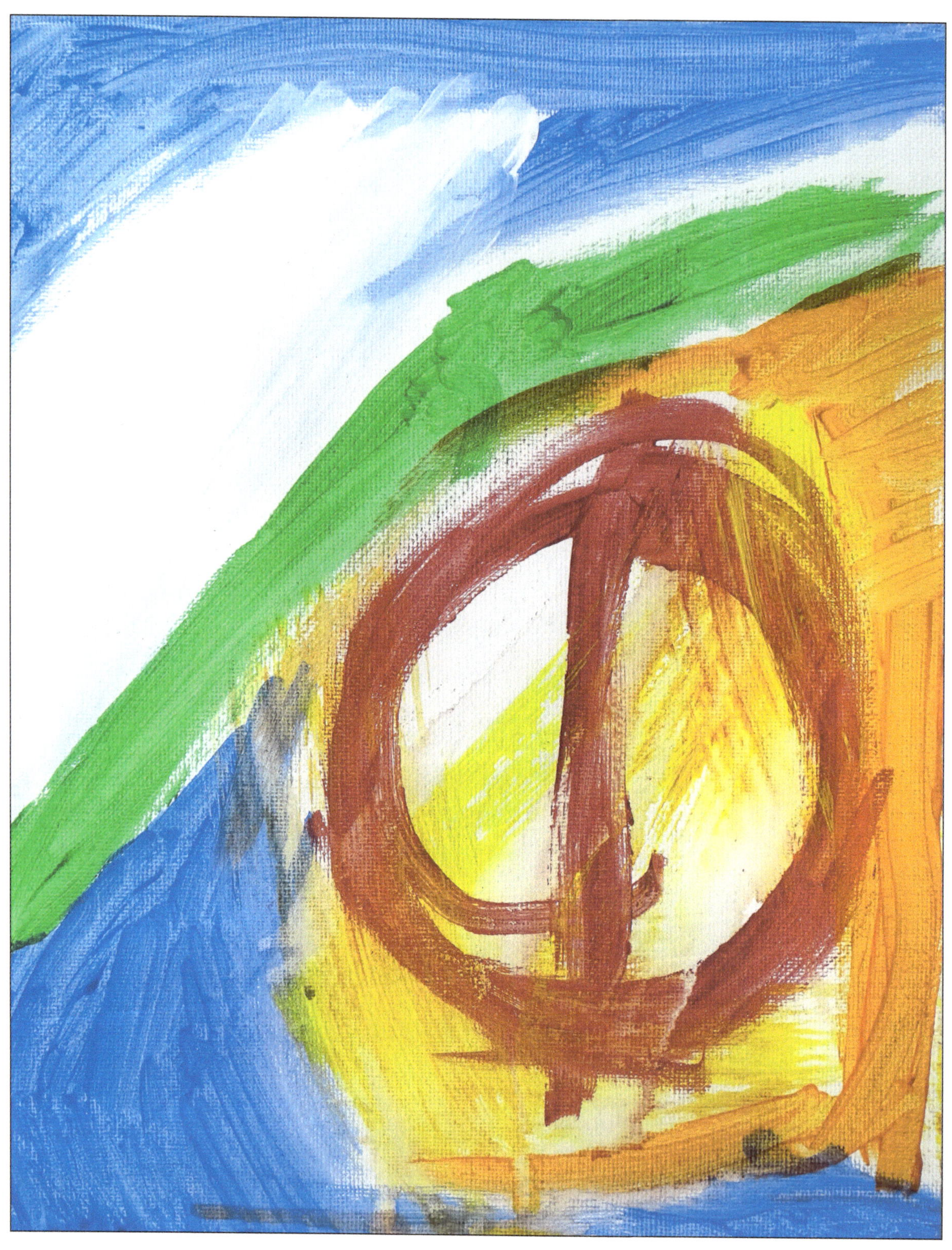

Circling

The epic setting—whispering in a flame.
of the circle—of the sky—and in life
Wandering setting—that falls into place.
Peacefully—silent midnight sky—and more.
Of this movement—of this circle—of
anything and beyond—and of this moment
circling—of that surrounding—like
creating itself OVER and OVER.
and in that Wild Life—and all these—
SOULS—like a beating drum—but with
reason—a beating drum is like another
real push of it's own—like your heart
that you can feel—OR IS IT SOMETHING MORE
than that? Like many many more—of the
Rain—that falls out from the sky—
Like circling a pair of eyes. Like it just
cries out of RAIN—and with COLOR—like a
big splash.

The Rain of silence—
Like breaking down,
tears of glass

and the whispering sky—
finally broke down

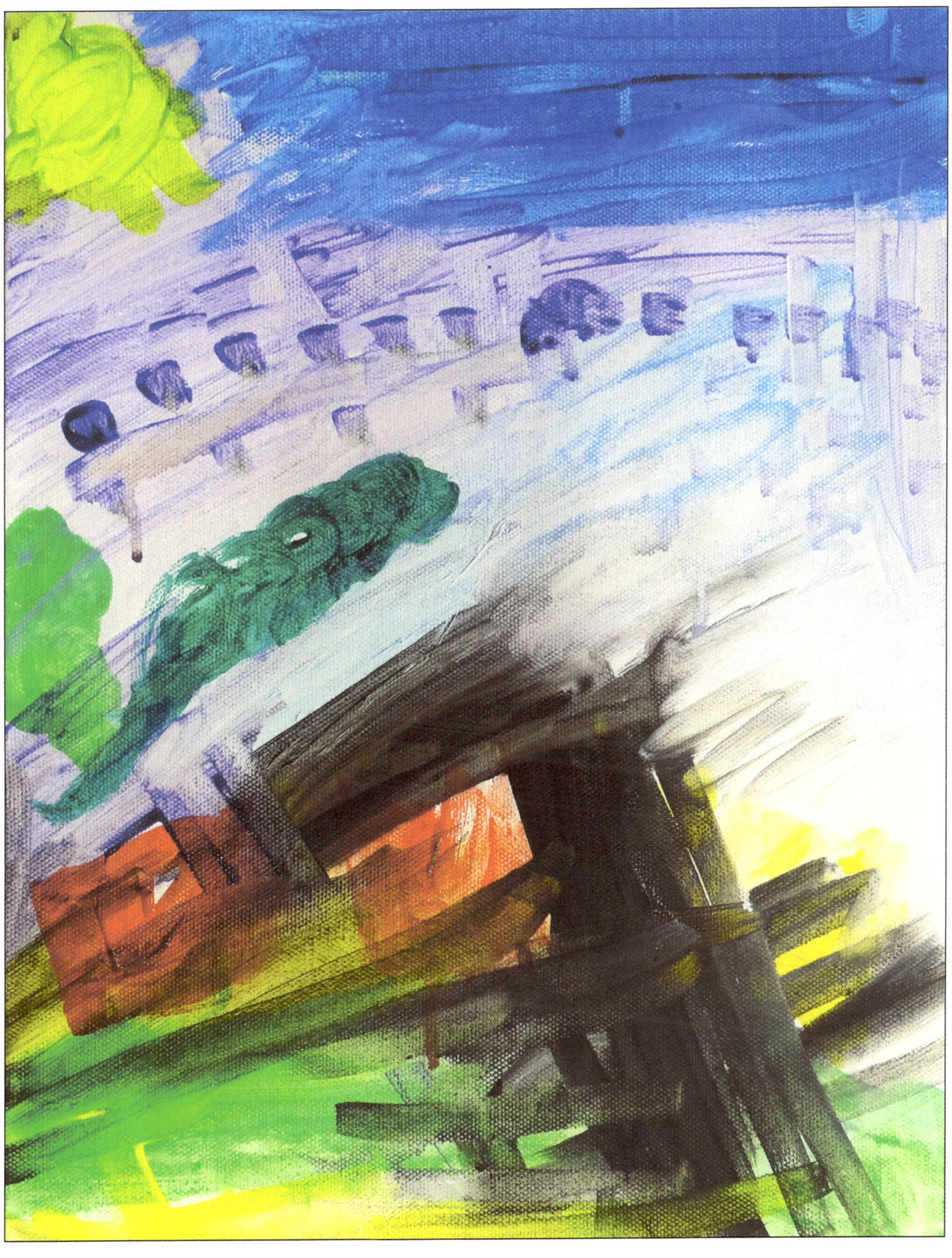

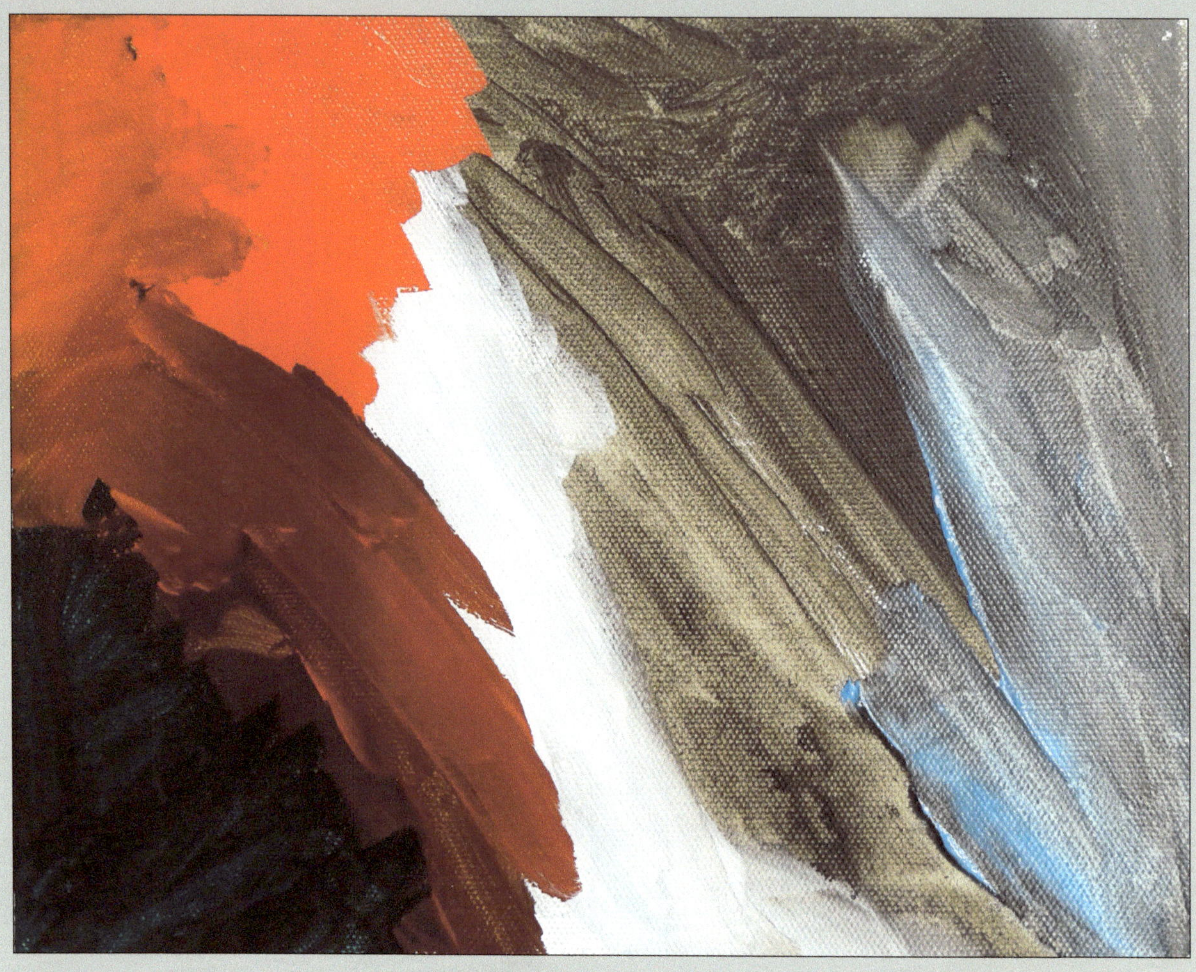

The Secretly Whispering Diary

The secretly whispering diary
Of silence. Silence like the dark
Of the blue moon—of this awakening slumber
And, likely, in my wrath and like many,
 many years
Have gone so quickly—or more?
More like this moment—like, unnoticed,
And likely, in this dream, like disguise,

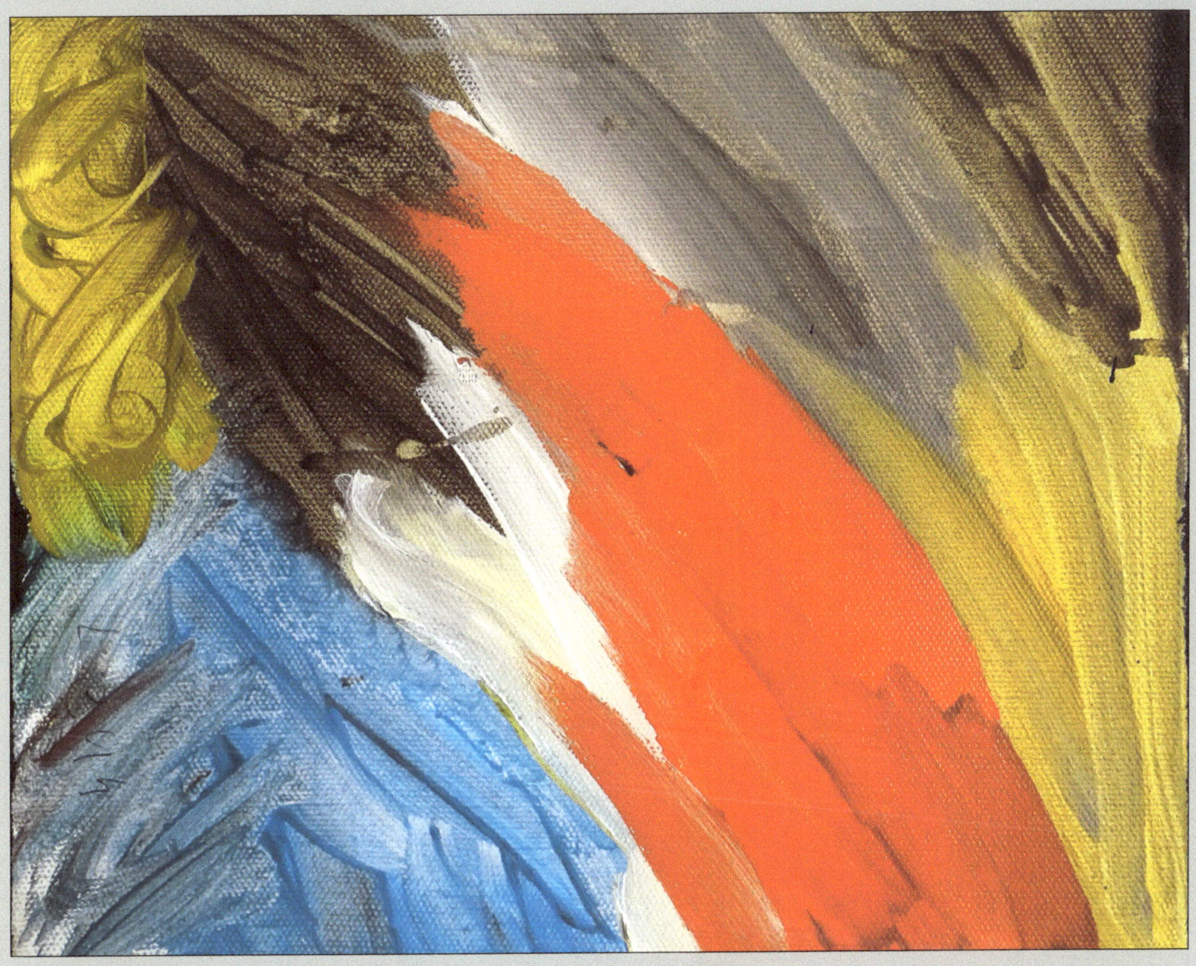

And with everything and anything that has
To come to an end. Or maybe it has to
be forever?
Like running and running into the dark
Or is it a dream world?
That you had never known before?
Or in this midnight time
Like it has to be like four in the morning
Here I am right now—with my own thoughts
Like in my head—like a memory
With this book that I call my "Whispering
burning out memoirs"
Desire that comes to and more in this
beginning of life
The life of mystery—and before—and now
In this life—like we have known before
Going to change—forever

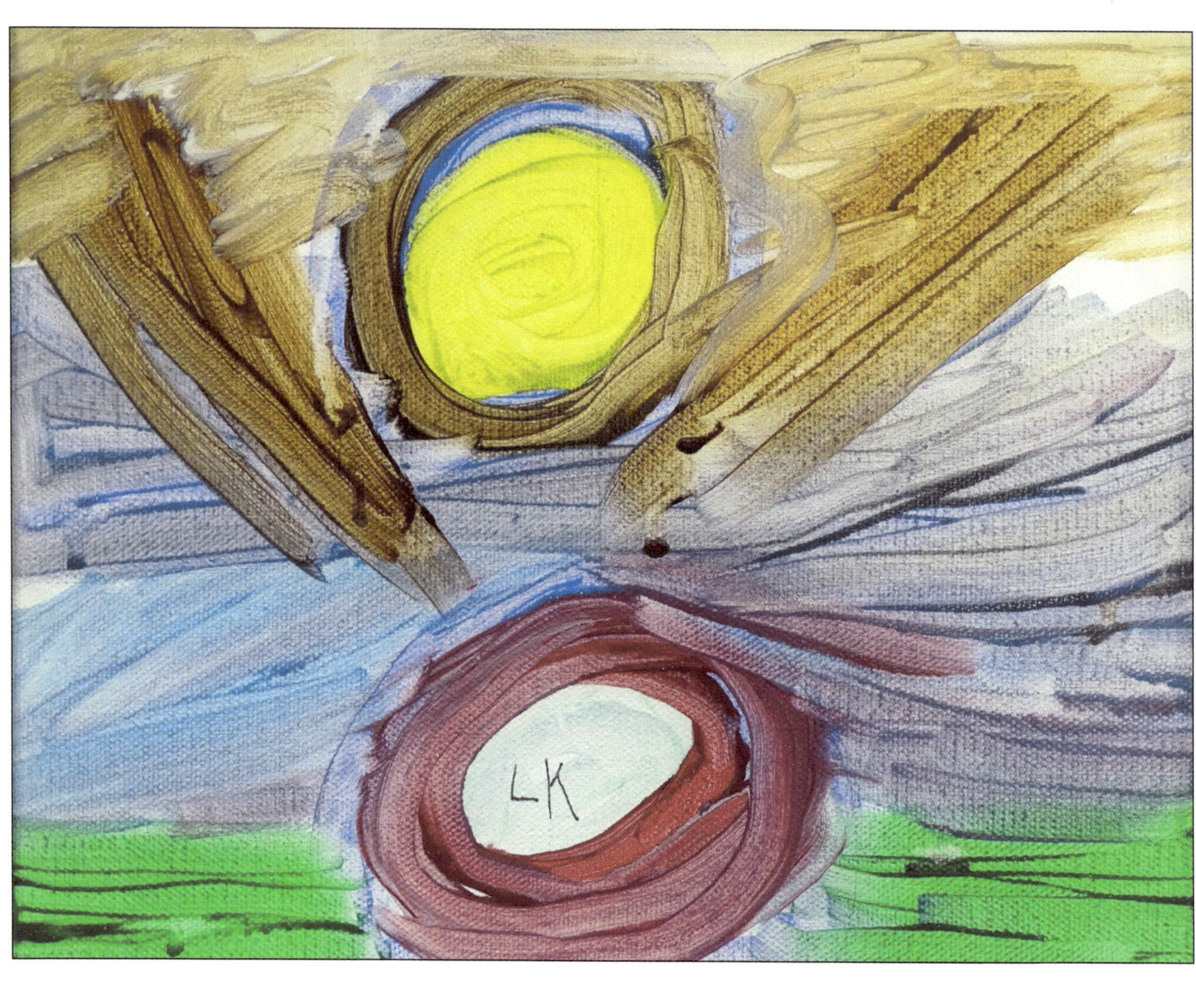
LK

Out in the City

Oh, out in the city,
picking up time—
but this was something so devious,
—like a pair of eyes—
like a surprise.
Picking up West
and the East Coast,
that lonely dog barking on the beach,
Sunny drive went high,
California—
with the birds going by: rolling, stolen,
picking up streams.
Those burning lanes,
so I drive,
and I drive—
out there in the moonlight cruise
with a prayer,
a prayer,
—a rolling stone Gypsy, rocking and angel in
the sky. My angel in the sky,
I reach out to you forever,
This is the way that I am. I've been
sleeping forever,
but finally have woken up to the broken doors
& the glass.
So here I am now, breathing out.
My eyes bleeding shut—
like my broken soul,
like pure of hearts,
wrapped so much inside of themselves.
But there are people that are not so like that.
Because they are more like individuals—
that were brought up in normal life, in integrity.
Sometime that I know,
or that I don't know—
can be so possible—or not.
That breaking,
but inside of this journey of a treacherous
setting of teardrops.
Setting of wonder in life that we know,
like of the discovery.
I am not saying it's possible,
or may be possible,
but maybe it's just like that continuously.
With open souls—
with a dirty piece of mind—
dirty, crafty, mind—
that I see, over and over.
Like a chapter piece setting through this cold
stone wall.
Competing over and over again.
Sometimes life is in itself,
or like the movement.
It's so sacred of a world.
People that are brand—new to the world can
bring us back in time—
To figure out anything that is so possible with
their own minds.
I'm not saying of any faults or claims about it,
or anything else—
of another piece of mind, integrity—
because that is just too controlling to the world.
For us, the movies—the new ones, that have
dirty minds,
that we have.
You cannot take that away, Because we
are going to tell you, over and over
continuously—
Because we are now here,
and we are not going away.

The Midnight Whisperer

A dream of silence
Like the fullest
Moonlight
of an awakening
Twist
In this moonlight
Slumber
of a memory
gone back in time
In the eyes of souls

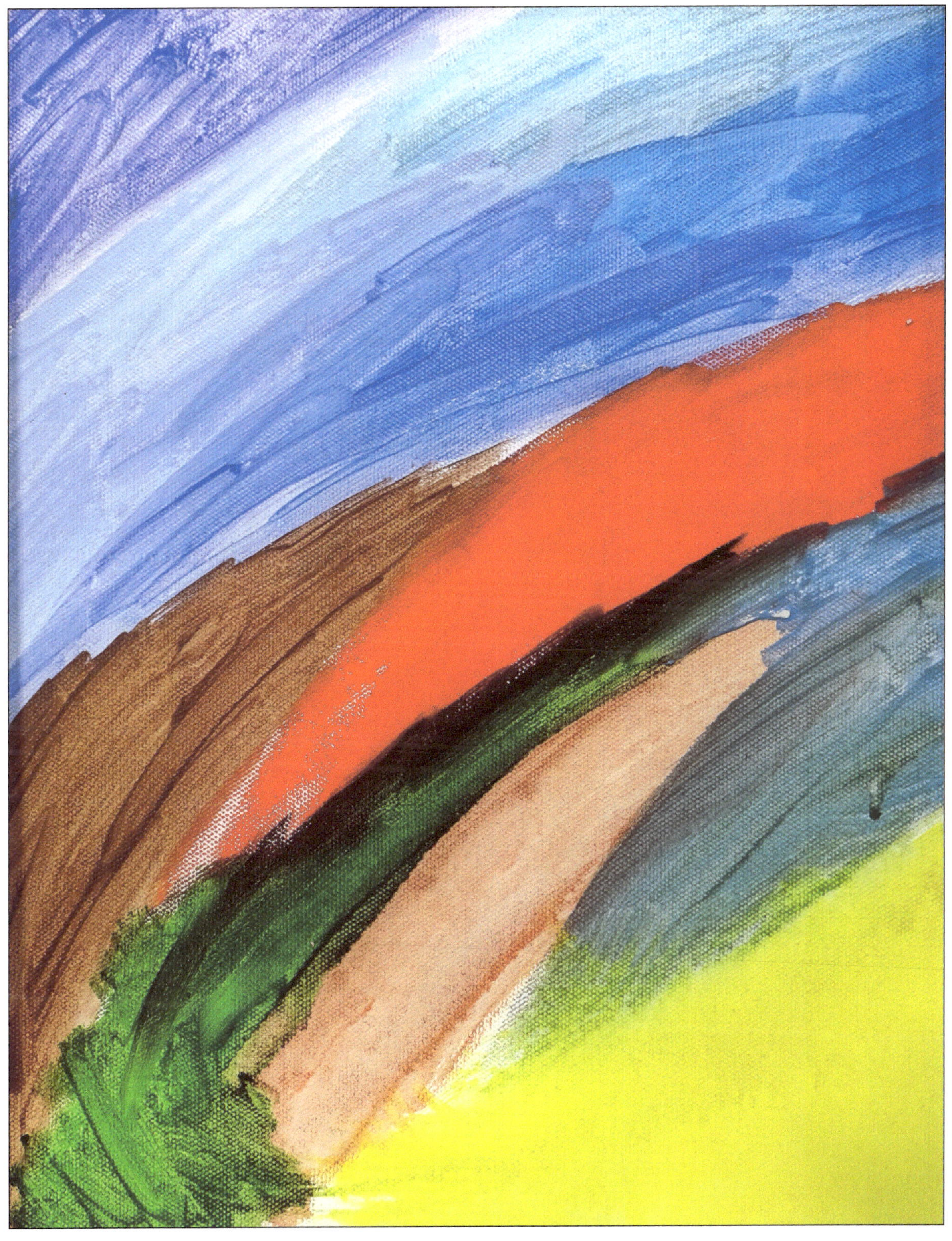

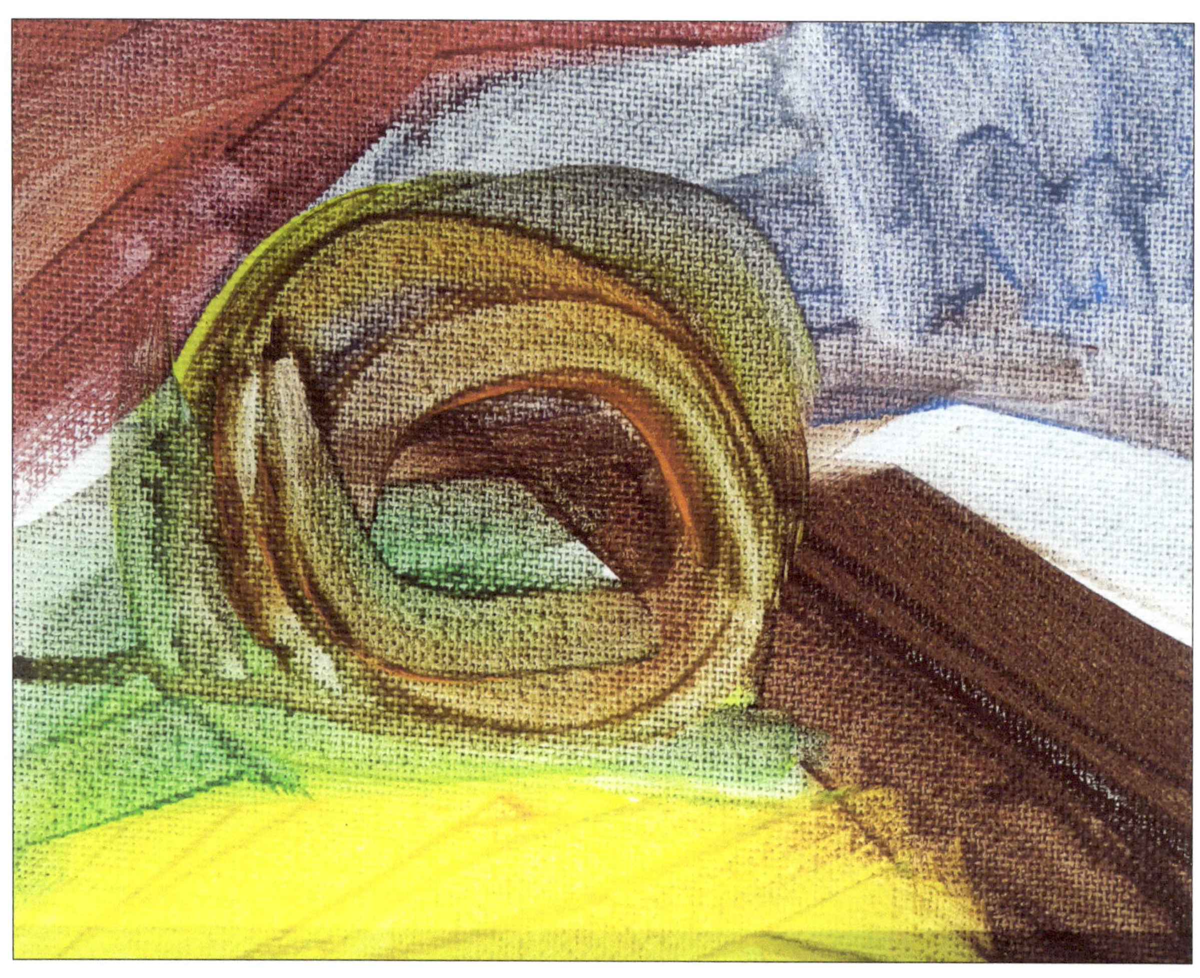

Beneath the Wings

The mystery of the wandering,
Circling of color and movement
And more to it—of the epic
Mysteriously of the rain that falls out, and in
So quickly, but slow—
And in time, like a dream
A dream, likely—
Like a twist, and of this new day
That's so much like the sun
The way it pops out,
Like from the moon—
Like it crumbles, but fades slowly
And like a fantasy,
Circling like a hole,
Whispering like the wind
That just goes everywhere, and falls into place
Like life—and all of this—
Like the wild life
And of this sunny, or is it a cold day?
Like nature—beneath the wings

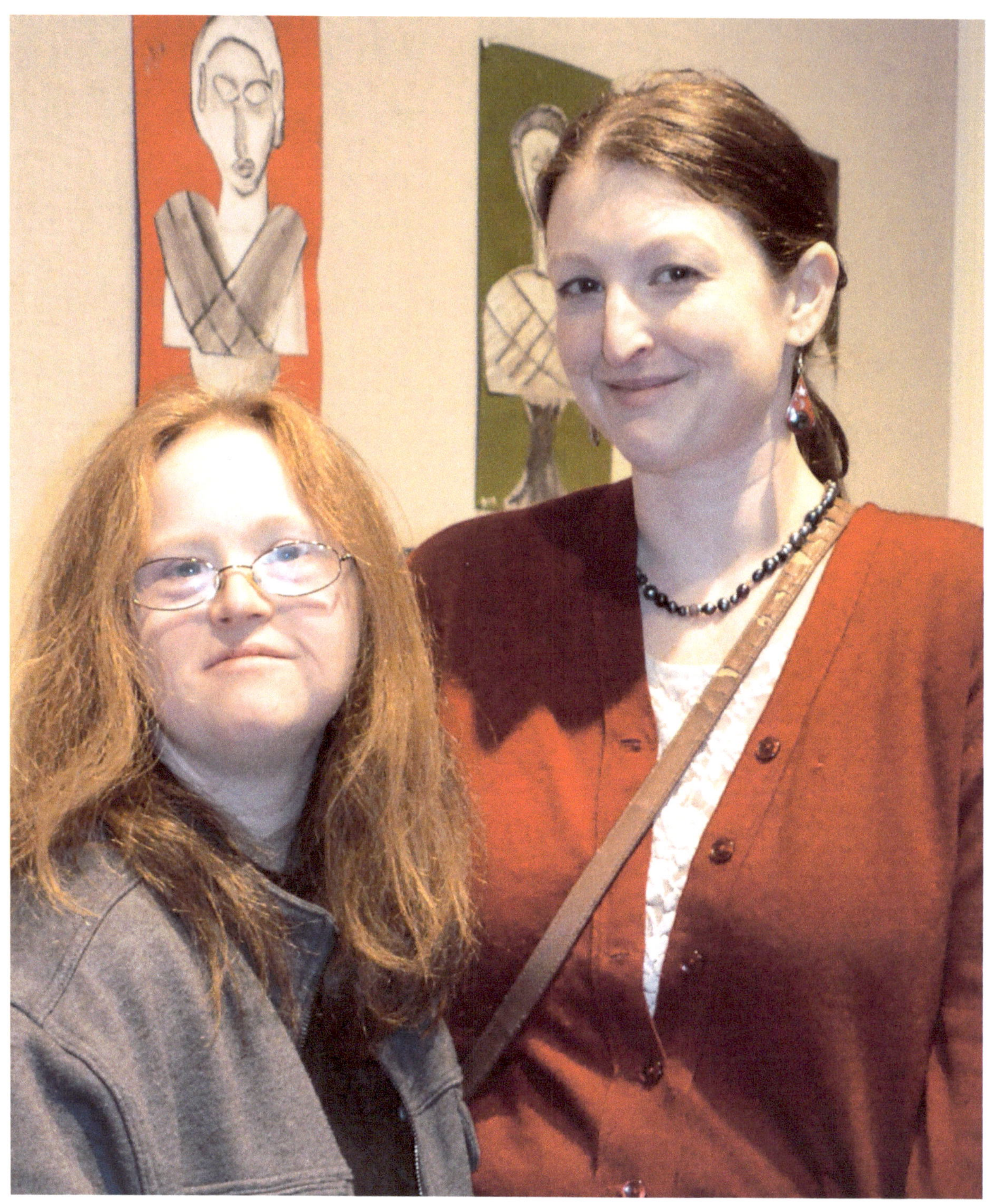

Leah and Melissa

CONCLUSION

The following was transcribed from an interview with Leah Keith on July 2, 2019.

Melissa: You received a grant from an organization that want to help foster creativity and artistic development. How do you feel about that?

Leah: I think it's really cool.

Are you excited?

Yes, I am.

Me to, I am excited for you. I hear you and mom are going to be meeting with some publishers. What's that process like, what kind of material are you gathering for them?

My writing and my art.

When you first found out you were going to receive this grant how did you feel?

Felt great!

Did you get into writing or painting more after that?

Yeah I did!

Tell me a little bit about that excitement.

Let me think. Yeah, so I started writing more and painting more because that's what I love to do.

Leah, what do you want people to know about you?

I have a voice, that I want to come out. I want to share it. I have a voice I want to share with everyone. My writing, that is my voice.

You're writing is your voice. That's beautiful. Your writing is a very vulnerable authentic part of who you are.

Yes it is.

It's a very deep aspect of you.

Yes.

When I read what you write I always feel a profound impact, it's very existential, it's very artistic, it's very colorful, it's very sensual, as in you are accessing many of your senses in a very in depth creative way. It is very impressive.

Thanks.

Let's break it down a little bit. There's how you feel about your work, about bringing your message to other people and then there is how you feel when you are in the midst of writing it and painting it. How you feel in that creative part of you, when you are just doing everything. So it sounds like in the first part when you were talking about how you feel when you get to share your message, it's very satisfying.

Yes!

And when you, because it's very important for you to have a voice and that your voice be heard.

Yeah.

And then when you see people's reaction and how they take your artwork. What does that make you feel?

Well, it makes me feel kinda good about myself.

Imagine you're in your studio, when you first start to paint or write. I'm really curious, how does the inspiration come to you, what's the spark that starts it? How does that feel?

It's kinda like having an imagination, just come out.

That sounds exciting!

Yeah!

If you imagine being in the studio at a time when this imagination starts to come out, what kind of feelings are you having?

Just good, it just comes out. It's kinda like, what is it? Kinda like a feel.

Kinda like a download, like a stream of consciousness?

Yes, that's what it is.

Is it almost like you don't feel as if you have to try or put a lot of effort into it, it's just coming through you?

It's coming through me yes.

That makes sense to you?

Yes it does!

I feel like that's the way a lot of really inspired artists have their imagination come through them. I feel that myself. When it's really inspired there's not a lot of effort it just comes through. It's as if you are in the most receptive mode in your mind.

Yes.

So that's kind of like the spark of your process, then you get really in depth and you start painting or you get into all the words and mom or Steve is translating it for you.

Yes, yes!

When you get into that flow, how does it feel for you?

It's kinda like a, what's the word, kinda like a meditation, I meditate and "Imaginate" and all that stuff just comes out.

Like an imaginative meditative trance where it just come out.

Yes.

That is really amazing, that must feel great!

Yes it does.

That must be really nice, it must be why you keep wanting to do it.

Yeah.

I am curious, because you have a lot of work you've done, how often do you paint right now. Have you gone through phases where you've done more or less?

I paint a lot, yeah.

You've been doing this for about ten years right?

Yeah I have yeah.

So in that time as it just been consistent, you've kept going every week?

Yeah I keep going yeah.

So how much time in a week, just as an estimate, do you think you're spending in the studio or just painting and writing?

Well I go to the studio every Thursday, so that's when I'm doing it.

So at least once a week at the studio. So when you're not at the studio, you often get into it at home.

Yeah I do, when I am in here (her room), at nighttime, I feel all that thinking that I do.

So at nighttime is when a lot of your juices get stirred.

Yeah, yeah, yeah, when I am thinking then that does that goes to my writing too.

That creative process flows into your writing.

Yes.

When you're not in the studio and you have a spark, and it's like 'oh I have to write, I have to paint!' do you act on that immediately?

Yes I do!

What do you do when you act on that spark immediately, tell me about it?

It happens spontaneously.

So you kinda go, alright I'm having this inspiration right now...

Yeah and it goes through me and comes out.

And you find your pen and paper, or the notepad, or the paint and the paintbrush and you just go right to it.

Yup.

Do you feel like there's a common thread or theme to your artwork and can you tell me about that?

Ok, I guess the theme kinda is going with the flow.

I noticed myself in reading your poetry and admiring your artwork that, especially in the poetry, there's a lot of theme of, well it feels earthy.

Yes!

There's a lot about observing the natural phenomena that happen around us.

Yeah! Because I think it kinda does, like what's happening right now, with the future and stuff.

Right. What's happening right now that might impact us.

Yeah like the future.

Because everything is happening now, and this is the future, right.

Yeah! (giggling all sides)

That's really deep Leah. So when you're really present and you're observing what's happening right now. What are the main messages you're getting that you're sending out to everyone through your artwork?

It's okay to be different.

Do you have any messages you would like us to share, that haven't yet been put into your artwork?

(Long pause to think) Some of my new ones too, that I have been doing, it's kinda like a scientific theme.

A scientific message?

Yeah.

Tell me more about that.

Like you know the wall with the circles on it? (Referring to the painting on my bedroom wall that Leah gave to me) That represents the future and how it goes on and just combines with everything.

That makes a lot of sense to me. I don't know if mom remembers this but there was a moment when I was about 12 and I had a very visual mind, I still do thats how I think. I know you can relate to that of course because you're my sister. I was just thinking about time and the universe and how everything comes together in a whole, a wholesome way and I said to her, 'time feels like, as if you were to drop a droplet of water into a big puddle and as the ripples keep going out and in and coalescing into one and other, that is time. That is the nature of time. It is not linear, the way we tend to think about it, It's on going and all connected.

Yes and it creates itself.

It creates itself. It is a self-creating process. And so that is what these circles represent in a very scientific and earthy way of observing the forces of the universe.

Yes.

I like that. From that, is there any other messages you would like to share?

Yeah, ok let me think. I have so many thoughts and I just want to bring that out.

You just want to bring that out and express it. And you feel like people should hear it because it will be valuable to them. Do you feel like people

are going to be helped by your work?

Yes.

Is that one of the main inspirations?

Yes it is yeah.

That you want to share your voice and help people?

Yes I do, yeah.

Is there a background, a part of your life you would like to share as part of this book?

Yes like a diary.

Right. So right now you can tell us about the parts of your life that have led you here that you would like included in the book.

My life and where it is. My life as me and having Down Syndrome of course.

Do you want to share about how having Down Syndrome is affecting your life?

Yeah. I am doing things and I'm going to keep doing it.

Yeah, you are a real person, you're going to keep doing things like everyone else. You're going to keep living.

Yeah!

Do you want people to have a little background as to how you got into these artistic expressions?

Yes! The writing I've done, I have been doing since I was very young. I have taken art classes for a while.

When was the first art class you took?

When I was in middle school.

What was it?

Kinda like ceramics. Pots, vases, plates.

So you got really into art through ceramics at first.

I took it in high school too.

You kept going with it through out high school and continued into college with different artistic classes.

Mom: when you both were little, I provided you with lots of artistic materials, all kinds of stuff, and I didn't guide you I just gave it to you and just let you create on your own. I think you both were very artistic, you know you both just wanted to write and create and Leah didn't want to do sports or other things. That was the thing she really took too.

Melissa: Another artistic expression that has inspired you your whole life is music. How do you think your enjoyment of music helps you transcend your messages into artwork?

Oh yeah, ok, let me think. Kandinsky.

Who's that?

He used music to help inspire his art.

So do you often listen to music while you're painting and writing?

Yeah I do.

And what kind of music do you listen to?

Oh let me think, Bon Jovi, now I am into music that's more like, well a little of everything.

And what kind of things are you listening to now?

That's a good question. I am into Journey.

So classic rock?

Yes.

Mom: Do you remember this? I had all kinds of instruments and different kinds of percussion instruments all around the house and Leah still has them all. We all used to use them and dance throughout the house every night.

What was the instrument, rainfall?

Melissa: The rainstick.

I really like that instrument because it was quiet and it brings out a lot of emotion and power.

Mmmm, it has a really subtle powerful quality, it brings you to a stillness in yourself that allows you to receive.

Yeah.

I wanna ask you Leah, whatever you would like to share, are there particular questions you would like to answer?

I don't know.

That's okay. I think you are a really deep intellectual person that uses a lot of senses to inspire herself and other people. I know you inspire me. And mom is painting a lot too now.

Yes she is.

How do you feel sharing that love and passion with mom?

Oh I love it, I love sharing it with her.

Do you ever paint together?

Sometimes.

And mom and Steve are the main ones who write down your poetry with you right?

Yeah they do yeah.

You must have a really trusting relationship with both of them.

Yeah I do.

Its a good foundation for your artwork.

Yeah.

Do you have any inspirations on the horizon for poetry or art that are coming out soon?

Let me think. Well you know that thing I did with Andy Warhol. He is an inspiration.

He's inspiring some of what you are doing right now. Tell me a little about that.

Well I like his work and I kinda found that an inspiration.

Tell me about how his work inspires you, what you feel about that.

Well I did that RISD class, that I'm still doing.

I do a lot of stuff there too. Is that class all focused on studying Andy Warhol or are there different artist?

No, there is a lot of different stuff.

Are there different mediums of art each week?

Yup, like stuff from Rome.

So it could be painting then ceramics another week?

Yeah like crafts.

On that note is there anything you would like to say to complete this interview right now?

Yeah let me think. I also do some things with clay. Making sculptures. I made one with dreadlocks hair.

You really like using your hands a lot, with the 3D art.

Yeah, yeah I do.

Thank you Leah. Thank you for doing this interview with me I really like hearing about what you are doing. I love you.

I love you too.

www.ingramcontent.com/pod-product-compliance
Lightning Source LLC
LaVergne TN
LVHW070129110826
845147LV00002B/217